Do Present

How to give a talk and be heard

Mark Shayler

This book is dedicated to Team Shayler:
Nicola, Daisy, Max, Tilly, Moo, Juniper.

Find your team. Let their voices be heard.
Together we are louder, together we are stronger,
together we are one.

Published by
The Do Book Company 2020
Works in Progress Publishing Ltd
thedobook.co

Text and illustrations
© Mark Shayler 2020
Author photograph
© Christian Banfield 2020

To find out more about our company,
books and authors, please visit
thedobook.co or follow us **@dobookco**

5% of our proceeds from the sale of
this book is given to The Do Lectures
to help it achieve its aim of making
positive change **thedolectures.com**

Cover designed by James Victore
Book designed and set by Ratiotype

Printed and bound by OZGraf Print
on Munken, an FSC-certified paper

MIX
Paper from
responsible sources
FSC® C163799

A CIP catalogue record for this book
is available from the British Library

ISBN 978-1-907974-76-2

10 9 8 7 6 5 4 3 2

CONTENTS

INTRODUCTION

Who'd have thought it? Who'd have thought that being able to stand up and present ideas would become a key business skill? Possibly one of the top three skills you need? Well, not me. I was merrily working my way through my university degree, majoring in drinking Newcastle Brown Ale and dancing, when we were introduced to a Presentation Skills module. I froze on this news. We all froze on this news. This was 1991. My history of presenting was not great.

While at primary school I'd go bright red every time someone said the name 'Mark'. This was the 1970s, there were at least three Marks in every class. My mates called me Mr Tomato as I blushed so readily. I hated the attention. As I got older things failed to improve. While I was really comfortable being the centre of attention in a small peer group, I hated the eyes, the expectation and the attention that a bigger group brought.

At sixth form, my then girlfriend started a debating society. A white South African boy called Jamie became a member and it soon became clear that we had very different views on apartheid. He was a defender of apartheid (I'd like to think that he has moved on by now),

I was anti-apartheid. Who wouldn't be? We'd already jousted in class. Then he said he would be up for debating it. What could go wrong? I had the moral argument, the social argument *and* the economic argument nailed. But ... I bottled it. I said I was too busy. Why? It wasn't that I would have a hard time or be proven wrong. I was just scared of speaking in public. I was scared. Shameful, looking back; I should have used wit, logic and articulate argument to change his mind.

Since then, I've trained hundreds of people to deliver presentations. Every one of them improved. The vast majority improved dramatically. During my presenting workshops, we film attendees twice — at the beginning and end of the day. When we film them at the start of the day I ask them to talk for one minute. Without notes. Or slides. I ask them to tell me who they are, what they love doing, and why they are on the workshop. Nearly everyone is nervous. Nearly everyone is hesitant. That's why they are on the workshop.

There is a general pattern:

People introduce themselves by what they do for money. By their job title. I'll come back to this, but it is nearly universal. This bit of their 60 seconds is the worst bit. The words are well-worn but not always human. Many revert to language that is valued (actually, I'd say *expected* rather than *valued*) in their workplace. These words are often a fabrication, a crutch, a prop to bolster self-worth and professionality. It can often feel like they don't even believe them themselves. This is when they sound the least certain, the least alive. I must add that this is about 60 per cent of attendees. The other 40 per cent speak eloquently and with warmth about what they do.

But we aren't what we do. We are more than that. This is why I also ask them to talk about what they love doing.

At this point people become more alive, more relaxed. It is as if they don't feel judged about what they love doing. Passion enters their tone of voice. Their body language changes and they physically change. The difference is (mostly) tangible. I say mostly. For some their work is their life, and the personal section of their 60 seconds, for a very few, is the most uncomfortable. But for most, they shine. We can all talk passionately and with authority when we talk about the things we love. That's why I include this bit.

The final bit sees them talking about why they are on the workshop. This varies. Some speak well already and want to shift gears. For the majority, however, they are dealing with a real demon, an ogre that sits in the corner of their mind and stops them becoming the person that they know they could be. My job is to remove that ogre, to tame that demon. We weren't born with it. Someone put it there. It may be that we put it there ourselves. But that's what is stopping you speaking eloquently in front of hundreds of people. That's what this book will do. It will remove the ogre. It will also give you tools, tips and structure to help you tell better stories.

About four years ago my eldest daughter graduated from Central Saint Martins School of Art and Design. We visited the degree show and her stuff was brilliant. An examination of the kitchen as a space where women have shared stories for centuries, and an examination of those stories. One of her mates, Kerry O'Connor, had a final piece on show that involved you picking up a piece of verse. I loved mine so much I've kept it. It relates directly to presentation and performance. I hide in the spotlight and this was perfect for me — and I think it will be perfect for you.

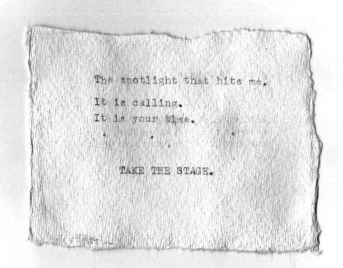

The spotlight that hits me.

It is calling.
It is your time.

TAKE THE STAGE.

The book is part workbook and part guidebook. Feel free to flick back and forth. I'm a real flicker; I tend to start at the back, I'm not sure why. But there is a structure to it and on first use it makes sense to read from front to back. You'll need a pen, some time, and a big idea.

WHAT ARE PRESENTATIONS? AND WHERE DID THEY COME FROM?

On the face of it this is a daft question. But, of course, it isn't. We can all talk with passion and openness. Maybe it's just in our family group (this is not a presentation). Or with our friends (this is not a presentation). Or with a group of people we just met in the pub (this is not a presentation). Or with our team at work (this is not a presentation ... or is it?) What about with the wider department/company? Is that a presentation? Yep, it is. As long as you're standing up. If you're sat down it still isn't a presentation. What about at a conference? Yep, it's a presentation. Office party? Yep, it's a presentation. Proposal to client? You bet it's a presentation. Project results to client? Yep, a presentation. I will just make it clear — if you are sat down for those last two, they are not a presentation. What am I talking about? Well, it's simple. When you are sat down, do you sweat and worry? No. When you are sat down, do you feel exposed? No. When you are sat down, it is not a presentation. That's why many of us choose to 'present' like this, hiding behind words like 'relaxed' or 'informal', muttering something about 'death by PowerPoint'. (PowerPoint and Keynote are beautiful. They let you put shape to thoughts. But only if you use them well.)

A presentation is when you project ideas to a group of more than one and you are standing up.

But you knew that, right? How did they get to be such a big thing, these presentation things? At university I thought my career would be about *having* ideas, not explaining them. Well, read that sentence again. They are the same thing and we have shifted from the written word to the spoken word as our main form of communication. Presentations are how we do everything now. A few things to keep in mind here:

1. **Does it need to be 'presented'** or can we write beautifully simple briefing documents that avoid filler sentences and gobbledygook? Apparently not. The quality of writing in briefings and reports, in bids and documents, is pretty poor. Too verbose. Too wordy. Too much business bollocks. That's why presentations are often used — to make things simpler and faster. In all things you do remember this:

WORDS ARE BEAUTIFUL, THEY PROJECT IDEAS. MORE WORDS ARE NOT MORE BEAUTIFUL.

2. **Present ideas, not information.** If it's the third-quarter results then it doesn't need to be presented. If it's a growth / comms strategy for the fourth quarter then it does.

3. **If it's not your idea or not a great idea, then don't present it.** Or make it better. More on that later.

4. **The idea is the main thing.** But a great presentation makes it sing.

5. **Being good at presentations is not having a big ego.**
   It is being good at presentations. It is not showing off, it
   is being good at presentations. It's a skill, one that you
   can learn.

A great presentation needs two things: Confidence in
yourself and confidence in your idea. We will work on the
latter in Chapter 7, but work on the former never ends.
This isn't a self-help book. But, of course, it kind of is.
The thing that is getting in the way of delivering a great
presentation is you. You can't be me and I can't be you.
For some, being on stage is being out of control. I think it's
the opposite — it is the most control you can have.

1
IT'S ALL ABOUT YOU

Who stole your voice? Who was it?

Because you had it at one point. It was there: in your throat, between your lips. You owned your voice. Then someone stole it. It could have been a well-meaning parent speaking for you; it could have been someone who knew that you had something great to say but they wanted to be the one that said it; it could have been someone who was so fearful of your power that they shut you up, continually (this is oh so common, particularly for women); it could have been a boss or colleague who wanted to keep you down (see the previous point — it's the same thing); it could have been you. Yes, you. Stealing your own voice. Keeping safe by staying small. We are not meant to be small. We are meant to be us-sized.

It's easy to think that great presenters are born, not made; that people either have it or they don't. This isn't the case. I can teach people to be good presenters. I can teach good presenters to be great. But it is true that some find it easier than others; that some actually enjoy it. These people are rare but you know one when you meet one. Most of them are like this in everyday interactions. They have charisma. Some, however, keep that part of themselves hidden. Like Eleanor Rigby who, as the Beatles told us, kept her face in a jar by the door.

The aim of this book is to pull that out of you, to give you the confidence to show your true colours. Cyndi Lauper says it best.

"*I SEE YOUR TRUE COLOURS ... SO DON'T BE AFRAID TO LET THEM SHOW*"

Songwriters — Billy Steinberg & Tom Kelly

Now I'm not saying that you need to be all showbiz, all light and no heat. Furthermore, this isn't a plea to bring a character out of the closet and become someone else. That's acting. That's different.

As I've already mentioned, the essence of being able to present with confidence splits into two:

1. **Confidence in yourself**
2. **Confidence in your idea**

You can get a good way through life, a career, relationships, parenting, by pretending to be someone you're not. But it is easier, faster and more effective to be yourself. Also, it saves time and money (therapist bills, sports cars, that kind of thing) to do it earlier rather than wait for your midlife crisis. This isn't intended to be flippant in any way. It is genuine. I'm fifty-one. I help people find a voice. I help companies innovate better. I work with companies on sustainability. I do some coaching. Through all of this I see that 70 per cent of the people I work with, talk to, that speak to me after a presentation, do not truly embrace themselves. This is in no way a criticism. But it is critical. How do you expect others to like you if you don't like yourself? How do you expect others to listen to you if you don't listen to yourself? Come with me on this. It can all sound a bit hippy and fluffy. But it matters and it works. I see the consequences. I see those that are lost later in life because they haven't sorted this stuff out earlier. This isn't about presentations alone. This is about life. Understanding who you are and what you are really matters. It matters to how you show up on the stage, in the meeting, at work, in life. We find it all too easy to slip on the overcoat of someone else, the uniform of the person we want to be.

I can't be you and you can't be me.

Those clothes are not yours. Wearing them is at best dressing-up and at worst fancy-dress. I lecture at universities. I do this for cheap/free because it is really important to stay inspired and connected to people who think differently to me. The problem is that while the students I lecture are undeniably smart, they are increasingly uniform in the way they think. They are the product of a system that values uniformity rather than individuality. Wider than that, they are the product of a society that penalises those that stand out.

I also work with some of the most innovative businesses on the planet. When the students begin to look for work, think about paying back their student debt (what have we done to our young people?) and getting a job they peel off even more of their individuality. They get a haircut, shoehorn themselves (metaphorically and physically) into 'business' clothes and go out hunting for work. The businesses I'm engaged with are coming the other way and are looking for something different yet all they see are clones of themselves. They walk past each other. Now, I'm not saying facial tattoos will be accepted by all, and I'm not saying that those big businesses won't try and mould the young people to fit their way of thinking.

What I am saying is that the most desirable skill that business needs (and arguably the planet too) is creativity. And yet, the majority of our education systems are built around uniformity, compliance, repressing self-expression and reducing playfulness. It is no wonder, then, that we hide who we really are.

Here is my little timeline of permission to be yourself, to use your voice, to express yourself. Forgive the shit sketch, someone once told me that I wasn't the creative one and it stopped me drawing for twenty years. Since then I insist all the doodles in my books are mine, rubbish or not.

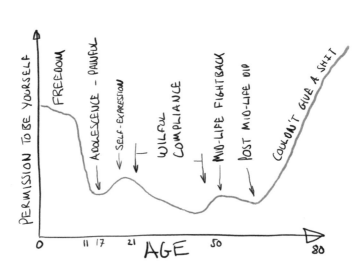

STAGE ONE: BIRTH TO 11
FREEDOM

Peak freedom is from birth to five years old. At pre-school you are wild. Everyone loves you and your eccentricities are not only tolerated but actively encouraged. This period continues to the age of eleven but as soon as you enter school your eccentricities begin to stand out. Furthermore, your parents spend time with other parents and will begin to shape you a little, to rein you in a bit. This is done out of fear. Fear that you will be picked on, fear that if they don't say something then someone else will. So, they rein you in a little because they want to protect you. They want to reduce the risk of you being laughed at. It is at this point that people begin to lose their voice. This can be as a result of a parent or sibling 'speaking' for you. Maybe you were 'late' to talking, so they step in on your behalf. This is about their embarrassment, not yours, but it is contagious. Maybe someone has a louder voice than you, opinions that are more forcibly projected than yours. Again, this is most likely due to them having to 'compete' for the airwaves at home. Whatever the reason, voice confidence can be dented at this point. The type of education system we are in matters here. Those educated in Finland, for example, are encouraged to be individuals first, to express themselves and play for longer than in other systems.

STAGE TWO: 11 TO 17
PAINFUL ADOLESCENCE

Now it gets interesting. Of course, not everyone has their self-expression wings clipped at this stage. Some people sail straight through. But for most of us, this is the difficult time.

A time when differences will be most harshly commented on. This is when so many of us lose our voice. It is when I stopped doing drama, when many of my friends stopped singing, when behaviour that doesn't align with the norm is most visible. It is when we begin to seek to conform. Now, I know what you're thinking, what about the weird kids? (I love a weird kid.) Well, like all tribes they find their own and create new rules of conformity. They are different together. This is not a bad thing. I'd rather be the same as my mates but different from everyone else than the same as everyone else. Standing out takes confidence but it is essential to self-expression. Please don't think that I'm talking about looks only here. You can look 'normal' but think different.

Tara Lemméy, a US entrepreneur, tech expert, designer and good friend, has worked with all the technology giants (yep, all of them, even the dead one) and she has this saying:

"ALWAYS BE TWO STANDARD DEVIATIONS FROM THE NORM."

I love this. Firstly, because I loved maths. Totally loved it (not arithmetic — that's different), I loved the beauty of replicating patterns, of not-patterns, of Fibonacci numbers echoing through science and art through centuries. Secondly, I've always felt like this. Just two standard deviations from the norm. I've sought it. The line has its origins with Frank Zappa who said:

"WITHOUT DEVIATION FROM THE NORM PROGRESS IS NOT POSSIBLE."

Undoubtedly true. But too far from the norm and you lose your audience, and even your friends.

STAGE THREE: 17 TO 21
A FLURRY OF SELF-EXPRESSION

For many, these are the university or the travelling years.
For others, they are the starting work years. Either way
there is space to play. This is driven in part by extreme
socialisation. We socialise more (usually in the pursuit of a
partner) and therefore are exposed to different viewpoints,
different styles, more bands. In turn this encourages a
confidence in self-expression. Some people enter this
period a little earlier (fifteen or sixteen) and others may
only be in it for a month or two. Being at university, being
in a city surrounded by diversity, undoubtedly provides
a broader space to play in, a greater palette to pull your
colours from, a bigger sound-desk to mix on, a larger
market to source ingredients from. You get the picture.
This age often sees a blossoming of self-expression and
voice. Good job, really, as what's coming next is bad.

STAGE FOUR: 21 TO LATE 40s
WILFUL COMPLIANCE

Our brains are at their peak from the age of 22 (ish) and
this lasts just half a decade.* It is at this stage that we
either enter the workplace or begin to take it seriously.
Yet it is the time when we willingly give up a little of
ourselves. Well, it actually depends *where* we are working,
but more often than not we will be in an organisation
that has usually grown through the phases of corporate
development or start-up growth and has an embedded
culture. This culture is shared between organisations,

* New Scientist: www.newscientist.com/round-up/five-ages-of-the-brain

has a language that is utterly baffling and serves only to shore up the corporate egos of the people within the organisation. Words and phrases like 'robust', 'traction', 'going forward', and 'from the get-go' proliferate. We talk in riddles. Furthermore, there are 'rules' around dress and what is and isn't deemed appropriate. When I was thirty, I joined a British supermarket chain as their Environmental Manager. This was in 1999 and in so many ways I didn't fit in, in fact, I refused to fit in. Unsurprisingly, I lasted a little over a year before I resigned.

Organisations shape us. The worst organisations, surprise, surprise, shape us the worst — actually this one wasn't a bad organisation but it was full of bad 'leaders'. And the worst leaders create a culture not far removed from the playground. They try to shape behaviour and self-expression in the misapprehension that they are creating culture. You can't bully culture into place, you can only set an example and give permission. Culture grows. Fear is at play here: fear from those above you that you will out-perform them; fear that being different is too risky; fear that you may be right.

Maybe you were lucky and weren't exposed to this corporate shaping (it's not just big businesses, by the way), but many are and this is where we can completely forget who we are. It's not that we become no one; it's that we become a character. Not a bigger version of ourselves, but not ourselves. This is dangerous. During this period you may be a great presenter, but are you being yourself or what you want to be seen as?

I see people at the other end of this tunnel as they escape the corporate confines (I do some executive coaching) and many genuinely do not know who they are and what they believe. This period is a long one and it can completely remove your identity. Those that survive this period intact do so by keeping a strong sense of self while still fitting in to the business. The secret here is to be lucky enough to have a leader who allows space to play, a safe space to express, and who isn't threatened by difference. These leaders do exist. Make sure you return the favour.

STAGE FIVE: LATE 40s TO EARLY 50s
MIDLIFE FIGHTBACK

This phase of life is well defined. It may come a little earlier or slightly later. But it has very little to do with work and everything to do with worth. While it is regularly considered a male phenomenon, it is broader than that. Stereotyped by sports cars, affairs and skinny jeans when you don't have skinny genes. These are attempts to find some meaning in life, to reconnect with the identity that you used to have. You may start playing old Joy Division or Television albums, watching Siouxsie and the Banshees videos on repeat. Perhaps even listening to Abba again. Whatever you identified with back then you will look for again. This is fine. This is healthy (affairs and sports cars less so — try yoga instead). Working out who you are really matters and will set you up to do some of your best work. The easiest thing, however, is not to have lost the essence of you in the first place.

Embrace your midlife crisis, see it for what it is, a chance to refresh and ever redefine the things you believe in. Use it as a way to strip away the inessential, to boil yourself down to what matters, to stop worshipping those unworthy of it and to be content with who you are. It isn't a midlife crisis, it's a recalibration. Use it, be proud of it, celebrate it.

If at this point you realise that you've journeyed on the wrong track for too long, don't fret. You can always change track. It's never too late.

As Bill Callahan wrote in the song 'I'm New Here':

"NO MATTER HOW FAR WRONG YOU'VE GONE, YOU CAN ALWAYS TURN AROUND"

STAGE SIX:
EARLY/MID 50s TO 60/RETIREMENT
POST MIDLIFE DIP

Okay, you've had your fun in your midlife crisis: now it's time to act older. What the fuck? No, stay young, ask daft questions, continue to be different. But at this point many people decide they are old, decide they are done. They are just waiting to be retired. Please, don't let this be you.

You may have enough pension to see you through to end-of-life, but have you made enough of a difference to see you to death?

Now, this is by no means a phase of life we all go through. But often the fear of losing a job and the challenge of bagging another one in your fifties is too great a fear, so you become the safe pair of hands and, often, the safe pair of lips. During this phase things go one of two ways: self-expression and voice are either reined in, or people enter the next phase early. I'm all for that.

STAGE SEVEN:
EARLY 60s/RETIREMENT TO THE END
COULDN'T GIVE A SHIT

And here it is. We have come full circle. But hey, that's life. Cue Elton and the *Lion King* theme song. We are back where we started with being truly ourselves. The meditations of later life are a great teacher. At this point you have nothing to lose and you can voice your opinions, bare your soul, be utterly open, without fear. My advice — get here earlier. Not to the moaning about your health and millennials bit (I know, I know, not all older people do that), but the zen bit.

So how do we stay *us* for longer? We deal with that in the chapter on confidence. You will learn how to believe in yourself and trust your voice. The key thing to remember is:

YOUR WORDS MATTER, THEY NEED TO BE HEARD.

2
LESSONS FROM THE BEST

**You know when you've seen a great presentation.
It makes you feel different or think about something in
a different way. It stays with you after it has finished.
Think about it: what makes a great presentation?
What forms the building blocks of a great talk?**

When I ask this in my workshops I get a range of answers:

— Engaging
— Lots of stories
— Confidence
— Charisma
— Relaxed style
— Structure

Yep, it's all of these. And more. But you need to master
more than one of these. You need them all. There is a great
short film (it's actually a spoof) by Pat Kelly. It lays out the
clichés of a TED Talk. It's really funny and really accurate.
When I first watched it I thought, *Shit, I've been rumbled*.
The video is brilliant because it's funny. It's funny because
it's true. The techniques that he's mocking *work*. That's
why he is mocking them, and he does it so well.

Adding a little laughing inflection to your voice when telling a humorous story works. It signals to the audience that this bit is light-hearted, that it is okay to smile and laugh at this point. Slowing down, talking quietly, signals that this part of the talk is serious, possibly even sad. I tell a story about the Democratic Republic of the Congo and the harm that is in all of our pockets in the form of tantalum capacitors in your phone. I slow down. I talk deliberately. I make you think about the implications of upgrading handsets early. I make people cry. The signalling is a big part of this. So rather than thinking I'd been rumbled, I realised that Pat Kelly's brilliant video is vindication of the techniques I use. You can learn a lot from a pastiche.

This book has an accompanying website where I've pulled together all the talks mentioned in the book so you don't have to spend time finding them online. You'll find the above talk from Pat Kelly and plenty of others worth watching at: **dopresent.co.uk/talks**

I'm a big believer in being organic, in letting things flow. But I structure the heck out of my talks. Everything is there for a reason. One of the key breakthroughs I had in terms of my own presenting was realising that just because I could do anything in my talks, I didn't have to do *everything*.

This realisation came after an event in Athens. It was one of my first paid-for presentations. I was opening an event and talking about disruptive business models (not the clichéd ones). I'd charged a modest fee for the talk. As well as the talk, I was also running a workshop the next day. Okay, maybe it wasn't the best rate for the three days I was there, plus the day spent preparing, but I felt lucky to be getting paid for what I love to do so I wasn't going to moan. Anyway, I was on first. I'd built a slide deck that matched the needs of the audience, I'd taken them 10 per cent further than they expected, I'd even worked in something from the Greek news that morning. I was feeling pretty pleased with myself as I sat down afterwards. People were saying nice things on social media (always a good sign but not the true litmus test).

The second speaker that day was a chap called Magnus Lindqvist — and he was brilliant. He delivered a presentation that was structured, surprising, funny and lively. He took the audience on a journey wrapped in stories. It was the best presentation I had ever seen. During the break, I went back to my room. My wife called and asked how it went. I said it was great but that I'd learned more than I taught that day. I explained about Magnus and how he was on an entirely different level. If that was the bar for professional speaking, then I fell a long way short. Then a text arrived. It said: 'Hey Mark, your talk was amazing, fancy a coffee? Magnus'. I finished my call and scurried off to meet him. He is one of the nicest people you could hope to meet, and he was really straight with me. He said that my talk was great but — as he knew the fee involved — that I had charged way too little. While I was left to run a second session, he was headed out on the next plane. This wasn't showing off. It was advice. He then said he wanted to help me raise my game. Now, I'm not going to tell you that he mentored me rigorously, or indeed at all. We met once after that for a beer. In fact, he never really helped me in any practical way ... apart from the fact that he did. By saying what he said, he gave me the support and the confidence I needed to keep improving — and to raise my fee. During his presentation I learned more about structure and craft than I thought possible. So thanks, Magnus, you helped me more than you know.

So, what were the things I learned that day?

— **Humour.** Being funny helps people to like you. Once they like you, they will more willingly travel with you.

— **Music/media.** While your talk shouldn't be a collection of other people's videos, you can use media to build a story and a point. Music in particular is very powerful.

— **Modesty.** Being good at something, excelling even, needs to be accompanied by modesty. Being human matters, and it matters to show it on stage. A little vulnerability goes a long way.

— **Structure.** The best talks are structured, even if they look like they aren't.

— **Help others.** Magnus didn't need to find my mobile number from the organisers and text me. Let alone spend an hour chatting to me afterwards.

———

LESSONS FROM OTHER SPEAKERS

ENERGY IS GOOD: GAVIN STRANGE

Gavin is a ball of energy. Really entertaining. Super-lively. He breaks all the rules. I suspect he always has. Most presentation coaches would advise not running around the stage. But for Gavin it works and it's perfect. He is utterly himself on stage. You don't want to wind yourself in, you want to push yourself out a little.

STORY IS POWERFUL: SEAN CARASSO

Sean Carasso is a gentle speaker. He told a beautifully paced story. The story of his life. He told us of hardship and then success. That's a great story right there. But then he told us how, during a period of his life normally spent partying, he built a charity. He told us the story of why he did that at the Do Lectures — and there wasn't a dry eye in the house. His storytelling, his passion and his controlled delivery was nothing short of a masterclass.

HEROES DON'T ALWAYS WEAR CAPES: MAGGIE DOYNE

Maggie gave up everything at the age of seventeen to build an orphanage for kids a long way away from her native USA. She did this with no knowledge or money. Her story was surprising. Her story was humble and she delivered it in that way. Probably the most watched Do Lecture over the last twelve years.

HUMILITY MATTERS: MICKEY SMITH

Mickey is a surfer, a film-maker, a musician and a Cornish-man. His love for the sea and the land of Cornwall shone through in one of the most humble talks at the Do Lectures. In 2009 he was the final speaker, and that's a tough gig. You have witnessed twenty or so blistering talks and the temptation is to change yours. Mickey didn't: he kept it simple and he crafted sentences that haunt me to this day. He then delivered a bombshell at the end that brought the house down.

OWN YOUR VOICE: HOLLEY MURCHISON

Your past grooms you for your purpose. Holley delivered a brilliant presentation at the Do Lectures in 2016. She talked of love, she talked of how what we experience makes us stronger and she talked about the strength to find and claim your voice. Holley's story is embedded in truth and honesty but what comes through is the fact that her voice matters; the fact that all of our voices matter, particularly those who don't normally have their voices listened to.

STORY BEATS TECHNIQUE: STEVE EDGE

Steve is flamboyant and a showman. So, expectations were high for his talk in 2010. And he delivered. He told a story woven together by mini-stories. I won't tell you too much, as we look at this one in more detail later in the book. The point I want to make is that although he stumbled over words and sequencing (these kind of mistakes are enough to derail most presenters), it didn't matter at all. His stories and his theme were bigger than his technique. And his technique was totally Steve Edge. He couldn't be anyone else if he tried.

THE 8 MOST COMMON MISTAKES

Codifying a brilliant speaking style is hard, as it totally depends on the type of person you are. Identifying and understanding common mistakes is easier. Here are the eight most common mistakes that I see.

1. THE SALES PITCH

Don't tell me you're funny, make me laugh.

I don't know who said that first, but I love it and I use it all the time. I think we've all sat through a talk where we are constantly reminded how the audience can buy from the presenter's company, about the range of services they offer, about the expertise they have. It is painful. It is unnecessary. Don't *tell* me how good you are — *show* me. If your work is brilliant; if you come across as human; if you are able to inspire the audience and assure them that you're good at what you do; that's the best sales pitch. The way we buy is changing. The way we market ourselves is changing. Presenting is marketing and as such it has gone through the same three revolutions that marketing has gone through. Mark Schaefer defines these best:

Revolution One: The end of lying. Doctors don't recommend cigarettes for throat comfort. Lying about your product or service and its benefits hasn't cut it for decades. Yet we still see and hear it all the time.

Revolution Two: The end of hiding. You can't hide any more. VW found this out to their cost. We can see everything now. A glossy story doesn't hide the fact that you don't pay a living wage, or are making excessive profits, or don't embrace diversity in your employment and marketing. We can see everything now.

Revolution Three: The end of control. Your brand is not what *you* say it is, it is what *we* say it is. Over half of your messages are out of your control.

I've simplified these considerably and Schaefer's book, *Marketing Rebellion*, is highly recommended.

2. RAMBLING

This is a challenge for me. I love to go off on a tangent. But what I've learned is that tangents must be curved (despite definitions to the contrary). They must come back to support your point. I play with the illusion that I'm on a tangent, knowing full well that I'm not. This works brilliantly when you bring it all back together. It makes the talk look effortlessly thought through. Once the organiser did intervene, though. I gave a lecture at a university and employed this tactic. I went off on an apparent tangent about the Stone Roses and the organiser piped up, 'Can we stick to the Circular Economy?' The tangent wasn't a tangent. It supported the main point perfectly, but I hadn't flagged to the organiser the fact that I would ramble a little. To be fair, I don't normally. People just trust me. However, if you are building this approach in, it makes sense to pre-warn the organiser.

But I mean non-intentional rambling. The sort that has no function or aim. In fact, it's a function of nervousness or lack of structure. Potentially both. When we are worried about looking daft on stage or being called out on the things we say, one response is to say more. To fill every second with words, to keep going so you can't be stopped, so you can't be challenged. To repeat what I said in the introduction: Words are beautiful, more words are not more beautiful.

By all means have free-flowing and unscripted bits of your talk. This is good. This is to be encouraged. But always have a point. Verbal scribbling is just a mess unless you can stand back and see that it wasn't scribbling after all.

3. LOOKING AT THE SCREEN

Okay, this is a biggie. This can ruin a talk. Actually, it's as bad as reading a talk out, because that's what it is. Slides are great. Pictures are great. Words are fine on the screen (more on that later). But they are not your notes. They are not to be read. They are to be talked around. Everyone in the audience can read. You don't need to read for them. Furthermore, we may have a 'best side' but I can be 100 per cent confident that it isn't the back of your head (unless you're sporting a killer haircut). You can't command respect when people are looking at the back of you. Look at the audience, it's only polite.

Think about your voice. Maybe you have a mic, but if you don't, you're talking to a screen. The audience are getting your voice bounced off a screen. Being able to hear you is a core part of your talk. So, stand central, talk to the audience. If you don't know the content well enough, if you have to read it; then don't give the talk.

Remember: You may have a beautiful behind but not everyone wants to see it.

4. SELF-DEPRECATION

The opposite of ego is not self-deprecation. It does not serve you to deprecate all over yourself. By all means be humble, but don't put yourself down. It is a classic opening gambit to tell a self-deprecating joke. But that's all you should do. Don't keep doing it.

The key thing about self-deprecation is that a little goes a long way.

5. THE COMEDY SHOW

I fell into this trap. It's an appealing trap. It is comfortable and people will like you. But it doesn't help you build authority. Please, please use humour. It is heartily recommended. Being able to make people laugh is a gift and it helps tell many stories. Just remember that you are not a comedian (unless you are), and that this is not a comedy show (unless it is). I'm funnier than average. That's it. I'm not a comedian. But I fell into this trap. Once you make the audience laugh, once you feel the laughter coming back, you'll find it is addictive. That's all good. Carry on being funny. But don't get confused as to why you're there. You are there to take an idea and spread it. Humour helps, but without the idea humour is just funny. Use it to do your job better.

I used to get confused about the outcome of my talks. I always went down well (apart from twice, but more of that later) but I clung to the feedback that centred around how funny I was, how much people liked me. Not how impactful my talk was or how I'd changed their business. Be careful. Humour helps so very much but don't forget the main thing. Remember that the main thing is the main thing.

You may be funnier than average, but you're not a comedian.

6. READING IT OUT

You know how it goes. You're a bit nervous, so you write your talk out word for word, you write a script, 'just in case'. You have no intention of using it, it is just a back-up. Don't. Here's a story:

When I started my career — I love the contradictory nature of the word 'career', it means both a work plan for life and being out of control — I wrote a publication for the Cyclists' Touring Club. It was called *Costing the Benefits* and it quantified the economic benefits of cycling to the UK. It was fresh research. Admittedly a bit niche. This was back in 1992–3 and no one had done this work before. The publication sold well. On the back of it I was asked to speak at their annual conference in my home city of Leicester. It was my first talk and I was dead nervous but I said I would. I had pulled together the research. I was speaking to a bunch of cycling nuts. What could go wrong?

Well, I designed beautiful overhead-projector foils (remember those?) and, 'just in case', I wrote my talk out. In full. I wasn't going to read it. It was purely back-up. However, the speaker before me was brilliant. Liquid, engaging, funny. He was a lecturer and knew how to hold the audience. Bugger. I stood up, I placed my foils on the overhead projector. I looked at the 700 or so people in the audience. Then I looked for my script. Then I looked up. Then I bottled it and read it out. Now, people were lovely afterwards but I was slightly broken and totally ashamed. I scurried home and tried to forget about it. However, a few weeks later a good friend and his girlfriend came for dinner. As they walked in, my mate's girlfriend was brandishing a copy of the Cyclists' Touring Club magazine. 'You made the magazine!' she declared. *Oh bugger*, I thought.

'Yes,' she added, 'and they said that Mark Shayler gave a very thorough read-through of his new publication.' *Oh bugger*, I thought (again). I do not want to be famous for giving a very thorough read-through. So, I never did it again. And apologies to the Cyclists' Touring Club.

Notes are fine, scripts are dangerous.

7. INTENTIONAL MOTIVATION

Being called a motivational speaker can be a curse. People say it with good intentions and kindness, and as long as you don't take it too seriously, and take yourself too seriously, then all is good. As soon as you see the motivation as the main thing then you are on a downward slope. Being seen as motivational — or worse, inspirational — is, of course, a compliment. The danger lies in believing the hype. I was once described this way, much to my wife's amusement. When it came to putting our young kids to bed later that night she declared, 'Dad will tell you a story tonight, it's sure to be inspirational.'

I've met many people described as Inspirational Speakers. Some truly were, both on and off the stage. Simon Sinek, for example, was like this. Others less so. One just had a series of stock images with motivational statements. For example, an image of a chain with a paperclip in the middle, over which he'd written, 'You're only as strong as your weakest link.' True, for sure, but repeating clichés isn't motivational. Telling your story, a story that lifts hearts and souls, now that's motivational. Tell your story, outline your idea, lift spirits, but do so with real content.

Don't say you're inspirational, say things that inspire.

8. YOUR LIMITING BELIEF

When I run my workshops I ask one question that I guarantee people will think about for the rest of the day and then take that question away and think some more about it, and will return to it again and again. I get emails about it weeks and months after people have done the workshop. What is it?

WHO STOLE YOUR VOICE?

First up, limiting beliefs are normal. We all have them. They are beliefs that we are a certain way, can only be that way; or that we won't achieve a certain thing, or don't deserve a certain thing. That could be really simple like, 'I'm a designer, I don't do business', or vice versa. Or it could be more fundamental.

You may have inherited your limiting belief. You may be scared of money or success because a parent was. Or maybe spiders or heights. Or you may think that your voice doesn't deserve to be heard. Just because your parent felt that. My guess is that some of you are having a penny-drop moment about now. That's to be expected, but remember that there is an expiry date on blaming your parents. Once you are an adult, *you* need to do the work. If you don't, these constraints may stay with you forever.

Limiting beliefs don't serve you: it's time to get rid of them. And hopefully by the end of this book, you'll have made a start.

3
WHAT DO YOU STAND FOR?

This is an important chapter. You may wonder why it is here. You may ask why what you believe matters to delivering a talk.

Well, in all honesty, you could probably deliver a good talk without this chapter. But this book aims to help you deliver authentic presentations. To be authentic, presentations need to have a few grams of belief in them. Actually, that's not enough. To be authentic, *you* need to have a few grams of belief in yourself. This isn't so much about presentations or storytelling, this is about you. This is about working out what you believe in and what you are 'for'. You will never start a presentation by saying, 'Hi, I'm Mark, and I believe that diversity makes businesses stronger,' but people will feel that through your presentation. Whether you call it a 'Why', a purpose, a mission, or a philosophy; I really don't mind. But it makes sense to work out what you are *for* as you go through life.

By doing this as people, we attract others who believe what we believe, by doing this as businesses or organisations, we attract people who believe what we believe. Indeed, it is more important than that. If we do it right, we will work with people who believe what we believe, and I can assure you that this makes for a simpler, more fruitful and more impactful way of working. In a world where competition is great, where markets are crowded, where big businesses are competing with no-overhead-third-bedroom businesses, your aim is not to be the cheapest. Only one company can be the cheapest. You need to be different. You need to stand out through why you do things and how you do things. Sounds idealistic, right? But think about your own behaviour. You will have your favourite tech brand, your preferred grocery store, your favourite soda, your chosen jeans brand. I would guess that you didn't choose these based on price. They were chosen because they were a good 'fit' with your beliefs and personality in some way. The way we define these things, the way we sense these things, is changing. In the past, brands used to tell customers what and who they were. Today we tell each other what and who a brand is. To enable people to understand our companies and organisations, we need to be clear about it too.

Research paper after research paper has identified that we make more decisions subconsciously than consciously. We intuitively know what to do, what to buy, who to trust. We do this because we pick up hundreds of signals subconsciously. We just 'feel' that we can trust this person, or prefer that company, or have a belief that is aligned with such-and-such a brand. In the old days people and companies would just *tell* us what they believed in. That's no longer good enough. You have to demonstrate it in some way. I say this phrase a lot and have already used it before in this book. I make no apologies for that as it is a great phrase: 'Don't tell me you're funny, make me laugh.'

I have no idea who said it first and Google is undecided; I do know that it wasn't me. But I use it loads, as it best describes where we are in terms of trust and marketing, in terms of belief and brand, in terms of friendship. Judge people on their actions rather than their words. I see the counter to this all the time. I see leaders extolling the virtues of building teams who do not have the first idea about teamwork; I see people working in the charity sector who display no kindness; and I see organisations talk about diversity then only use skinny white models in their campaigns. The thing is, you can't hide this stuff any more. How you behave must be aligned with your beliefs, and your beliefs have to align with your words. As I say, you will never (or rarely) state your beliefs upfront in a talk, but people will *feel* the kind of person you are and they will decide whether to trust you (or not).

It is therefore essential to work out what you are for and what your company is for. This will be the backdrop, the North Star, the mood music, to your presentations. In fact, it is much more important than that: this will be the backdrop or the North Star to your life.

Many people define what they stand for by defining what they are against. This works. This is perhaps the easiest way to determine what you believe.

One really simple exercise is to write out all the things you are 'against' on the table that follows. I encourage you to go really wide here before you narrow in on your chosen field or area of work. It could be anything: fossil-fuel use, Big Pharma, a society that fails to value free healthcare, racism, misogyny, all of the above. Write them down in the 'I stand against' column on the left.

Then in the middle 'Why these things are bad' column, write down why you stand against them. Then I want you to write in the third 'Where I see them' column. This could be a list of brands, competitors or people. There is no judgement here, we are all on a journey.

I STAND AGAINST	WHY THESE THINGS ARE BAD	WHERE I SEE THEM

Once completed, the table will show what you stand against. It can really help if you're struggling to define what you stand for.

Now I want you to sharpen your pencils and minds and crack on with the second table over the page. This is the 'What I Stand For' table. It too has three columns. The first column is simply 'I stand for' and I would like you to write the things you believe in, the things you value more than others. As a starting point, you can use the 'I stand against' column and write down the inverse of these. Or you can start with the list of values in the Appendix at the back of the book and write down those that resonate most strongly with you. Aim for five things. Write them in the table. Then shift on to the middle 'Why these things are good' column. This is all about impact. What positive differences do these beliefs produce? Why do they make people's lives better? Why do they matter to customers? How can they improve business? This column is general rather than specific. Finally, I want you to write down specific lived examples. Ideally these will come from your life, from the work your company has done, from the mouths of your customers. What examples can you use to bring the benefits of the things you believe in to life?

Now this is where it can get a little tricky. You may not have any examples. What then? In that case, you can use examples from other people or organisations. This isn't stealing, as you're not going to pass them off as your own (that *is* stealing). You are just going to use them to make a point and you will credit the story to the originator. One example I use is that of British fashion designer Paul Smith, who immerses himself in the culture of wherever he is when travelling. When he arrives in a new city or country, he immerses himself in the sights and sounds of the new place. He takes his headphones off, puts his phone away, takes public transport or walks the last bit of his journey from airport to hotel. He walks the streets, smells the air and tastes the culture. I use this example to illustrate the point that a designer's greatest skill is observation and imagination rather than drawing or CAD, and that feeds back into one of my beliefs that observation is more important than rushing to an answer. This isn't *my* example, even though I do the same thing. No one really cares how I get my ideas. They do care how one of the most successful designers on the planet gets his. You can shore up your beliefs by leaning on the behaviours of others, just as long as you are honest.

Now you will have a list of things you believe in, the benefit they bring to you / your life / sector / business / world, and a few examples. And it's the examples that you will air rather than the beliefs.

It's easy to dismiss this stuff and ram your presentation with information on price, financial benefit and hard selling. The only one of these that matters is the middle one. But if you take a more elevated approach and make it clear why you do what you do then people will come to you.

It is a hackneyed (and old) talk now but a good reminder is Simon Sinek's 'Start With Why'. People don't buy what you do, they buy why you do it. As I said earlier, only one company can be the cheapest: the rest have to be different and better. Sure, his main example, Apple, is a very different company now, but that really proves his point. When Apple was led by Steve Jobs its 'Why', its purpose, was clear. Today it isn't. His example still stands and you can find his TED talk on the book's website.

Despite being filmed in 2010, I still use this exercise today. Why? Because there is still nothing as good at differentiating between the Why, the How and the What of what you do. To summarise, everyone knows what they do,

I STAND FOR	WHY THESE THINGS ARE GOOD	LIVED EXAMPLES
—	—	—

some people and organisations know how they do it (this is a differentiator), but very few can explain why they do what they do; the most successful organisations are able to do this clearly. I recommend following his process — it works. You can find out more from his own website *simonsinek.com* but the simple exercise I use is to write down your Why as a belief statement:

I/WE BELIEVE

....

....

....

....

IN ORDER TO

....

....

....

....

The risk is that you gravitate towards explaining what and how you do things. Think like a hippy, think like an idealist, embrace that side of you when writing your purpose or Why statement. There's loads of time for realism later. The second sentence grounds you, drives you to think about the consequences of what you do and why you do it. It is as important as the first bit. This isn't easy, and it will take a few goes. A simple way of checking if you are headed in the right direction is to ask 'Why' of your statement. If you can go further back then do so. Here is an example:

I asked a friend what her Why was. She responded with, 'I believe in delivering great dinner events.' Okay, the eagle-eyed among you will spot that this isn't a Why. So I asked why she believed that. She said that eating together is better than eating alone. Yep, but still not a Why statement. So I asked why again. She replied that eating together allows you to share ideas. Yep, agreed, but I wanted more. We got there in the end. She believed that being together spreads greater understanding and grows better ideas. She brings people together in informal groups and the way she does that is through food.

The best way of demonstrating what you are for is not in a statement but in a story, in the work you do or the things you have done. This is also the best way of 'selling' too. No one likes a heavy seller. If you're good, if you explain the work you do by talking about the difference it makes, if you come across as believable and honest, you won't need to chase work. Work will chase you.

———

I always start my talks with one of three stories. These are things that happened to me in real life. One is about taking my primary school out on strike over the school dinners, one is about believing I wasn't creative and couldn't sing, and the third is about refusing to move South African apples during the apartheid era. This last one also resulted in a strike. I use these stories to add texture to the point I'm making. These points are, respectively:

— **With power comes responsibility;**

— **We are all creative;**

— **If you stand for nothing you'll fall for anything.**

They also go a long way to build a picture of the things I believe in: Kindness; Creativity; Equality. They are inextricably woven in to my Why / Purpose and there is no avoiding the kind of person I am. I don't need to tell you, I just tell you a story. I don't need to state my mission, you can feel it.

Your purpose will attract people to you. Well, it will attract people who share that purpose to you. It will repel those who don't agree or understand. To my mind that is equally as useful. Being vanilla has, in my experience, led to more bad things than good. Your purpose will sit, like a backdrop, behind your presentation. Don't labour it, don't push it too hard. It is like a subtle perfume rather than a harsh air freshener. It is important for it to permeate gently, to infuse rather than overpower the audience.

Be careful: if you don't mean it, if you have made it up, if you don't honour it with your behaviour, people will find out. The truth is not just out there, it is easier to see than ever before. Being inauthentic about your purpose is worse than not having one at all.

4
SPREAD IDEAS, EXPAND MINDS

At a time when it is easier to live in isolated bubbles than ever (well, since before the horse and the bicycle allowed us to travel out of our immediate neighbourhood) it is increasingly important to share ideas. Presentations spread ideas. That's what they are for.

Sure, you may be asked to deliver a presentation that updates Q3's sales figures. Some things shouldn't be presented. Sharing ideas about Q3's sales initiatives — that is worth presenting.

If you don't have an idea then why are you presenting? If you don't have an idea that will shift something in the audience then why are you presenting? Just because you can, it doesn't mean you should. Presentations are powerful but we weaken their power when we over-use them. We weaken their power when we use them to spread information, not ideas. Information is the past, ideas are the future.

I liken this to the difference between data and insights. Both matter. And one can give rise to the other. But one is history and the other is the future. Data is what has already happened. Data can help predict the future, but imagination can shape it. I'm not saying that data and information don't matter. They really do. But pulling the meaning from data, the trajectory from information, that's where the magic is.

Present ideas, back them up with data.

HOW TO HAVE BETTER IDEAS

So, I'm going to talk you through four things I do to have 'better' ideas. When I say better, I mean ideas that are less obvious, more insightful; ideas that excite you and fill you with energy.

1. ASK A BETTER QUESTION

Sounds easy, right? Just ask a better, more stretching, more challenging question. It's actually really hard. The natural instinct is to pull our horns in a little, to lower our expectations when we seek new ideas. We tend to gravitate towards what we already know, to the thing we did last time, maybe with the addition of 'How can we make it a bit better?' Or, 'What are our competitors doing, let's do that!' The first of these gives rise to ideas that are sequels. This is where Apple are now. Incremental improvement. They used to ask better questions. I'll sum up the problem with this approach with a clumsy analogy. The film *Police Academy* was funny. The film *Police Academy 7* was neither funny nor demanded by the public. Great ideas rarely come in sequel mode. The same is true for copying competitors. By all means get inspiration from others, but taking what someone else has done and making it a little better is not having a new idea. Try asking a better question.

2. STAY IN THE PROBLEM FOR LONGER

While developing ideas fast is all the rage, there is a lot
to be said for sitting in a problem for longer. Rushing to a
solution too soon can sometimes result in developing the
most obvious rather than the best idea. Patience during the
observation and idea-generation phases often produces
better results. After that, by all means sprint away.

So sit in the problem for longer; sit in the discomfort of
the problem for longer. Einstein supposedly said, 'If I were
given one hour to save the planet, I would spend fifty-nine
minutes defining the problem and one minute resolving it.'
Many mistakes are made by solving the wrong problem.

3. MEDITATE

What? Yep, meditate. When we meditate our brainwaves
change. We are at our most creative / inventive when we
are in a 'theta brainwave' state. This is the brain-state we
experience just before sleep or during repetitive activity
such as running, swimming and, more alarmingly, driving.
These brainwaves are slow. When we're in this brain
state we are prone to a greater flow of unedited ideas.
This is a free-flow state and we can also enter it when
showering, gardening or meditating. I'm guessing that the
majority of you meditate (if not, why not?) and therefore
you will be aware of the benefits of a calm mind. But you
can use meditation to spark ideas too. Both Einstein and
Edison used meditation as a way of switching to a more
creative mindset. Allegedly (and I really hope this story is
true), Thomas Edison would fixate on a challenge while
meditating in order to crack a gnarly problem. He would
write down the problem on a sheet of paper — how to
make a better lightbulb, for example. Then he would sit in

an upright chair next to a table with the paper and a pen on it. He would pop a metal cup between his feet and hold a coin between his knees. Then he would meditate. As he relaxed, his brainwaves shifted from beta (highly charged and totally awake) to alpha (mentally active but not as focused) to theta. The one after theta is delta (sleep), so as he slipped through theta to delta he would naturally begin to fall asleep. His knees would relax, the penny would drop (yep, that's the origin of the phrase), land in the metal cup and wake him up. He would then write down whatever he was thinking about. Genius. But then he was.

So, how can you be more Edison? Find your meditation. It doesn't need to be namaste-style meditation: it can be gardening, walking, knitting or running. Anything that shifts you into a more hypnogogic, almost trance-like state. Get used to switching off to get better ideas. As my swimming coach says, 'Slow down to go faster.' True that. Swimming is a form of meditation that I've only recently discovered and I can't recommend it highly enough. I dive in and love the prickle on my skin as the temperature change registers. I love hearing the sound of the above-water world muffle and fade away. Then it's just me. Underwater. I dolphin-kick for half a length and stay down swimming as far as I can until I need to breathe. Until my lungs are screaming for oxygen. Then I stay down a little while longer. Surfacing, the first breath has never felt as good. This is a meditation. It is also a ritual. We talk about ritual later in the book. Find a meditation, find more ritual in your life.

4. IDEAS GENERATOR

There are many ways of generating ideas and hundreds of tools to help you. You will probably have your favourite and if you have, my advice is to use the one you like the most. But if you haven't got one you use regularly, here's mine. It may help. It's called Mark's Idea Daisy.

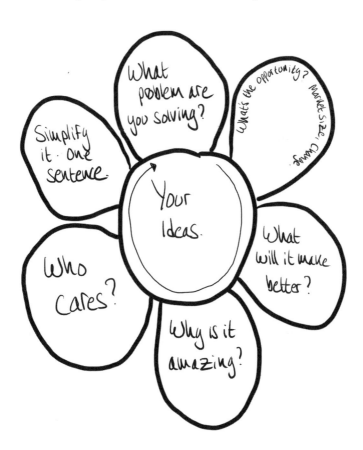

I start in one of two places. I either start with an idea (if I have one) or more often I start with a problem. Starting with something that irritates the heck out of you is a good place to start because you're already invested. It may be a problem you see at work or one that you see in life generally. It may be a problem you care about or it may be a problem someone else has observed. The process is the same. Look at the problem and ask yourself, 'Why is this a problem?'; 'Who is it a problem for?'; 'Why hasn't it been solved before? What thinking has failed us?' Defining the problem like this is a great way of sitting in the problem for longer and stops you rushing to the obvious solution. I then work around the daisy in a clockwise direction and every time I think of an idea I write it in the middle. I answer the question in each petal for each idea. A favourite will emerge (but don't throw the others away — their time will come). The petals are comprised of the following questions:

1. **What problem are you solving?** The key elements here are: Why is this still a problem? Who experiences the pain of the problem the most? What thinking has failed us? How can we redefine the problem?

2. **What's the opportunity?** Long gone are the days when we measure opportunity only by money. But money still matters. If you're not making a profit then you're not a business. So, what is the financial size of this opportunity, just roughly; and then what is the human size of this opportunity? What level of change can it bring? To you, your business or the world? Why give a presentation if it doesn't make a difference?

3. **What does your idea make better?** Whose lives does it improve? What are the social benefits? What are the efficiency benefits? What are the business benefits?

These are non-financial benefits and they can be really broad.

4. **Why is it amazing?** There are two things I'm interested in here. First, why does this excite you? Why does it make your socks go up and down? Second, why do you have an unfair advantage here? Why are you the best person or organisation to do this? Why is it only you / your business who can make this work?

5. **Who cares?** Genuinely as simple as that. Who cares about the idea? Are the audience those people? If they aren't — how can you bring this issue to life so that they become people that care about this? Or advocates for what you are doing? You're looking to create a little Velcro so that your idea sticks to them.

6. **Simplify it.** We all live in a language bubble. We all use language that relates to the world we live in. This assumes a certain level of knowledge and it is easy to slip into this talk when we present. So keep things simple. Not just the terminology but also the idea. Boil it down to its simplest form.

My guess here is that you might like an example?
So here goes.

What's the problem I'm solving?
Bad breath. Not mine, but my dog's. My dog Ralf died this year. He was a Jack Russell and towards the end of his life his breath got bad. Really bad.

But that's not the real problem. It's always worth digging down a level. The problem with a dog with bad breath is that no one wants to stroke them. So they feel unloved. But that's not the only problem.

When we stroke a pet there are health benefits. Our heart rate and blood pressure can fall and it releases a relaxation hormone, and can help with PTSD. So actually the problem is that canine bad breath equals more stressed humans.

What's the opportunity?
In numbers: there are 9 million dogs in the UK, and 26 per cent of UK households own dogs. That's a big market and a large number of lives to impact.

What does this make better?
Being able to get closer to your dog as it ages will clearly improve the dog's quality of life. But, as discussed above, it will improve the owner's quality of life too. It could also cut down on the amount of air freshener you buy.

Why is it amazing?
Love until the day you die! Need I say more?

Who cares?
All dogs and all dog owners and their families and guests.

Simplify it
A dog is for life (not just until it starts to smell).

So what are my ideas? First, dog toothbrushing every morning and evening. Yeuch, not a winner. Second, dental chew-sticks — they clean teeth but don't smell great. Third, mint-flavoured dog food. Sure, it's a rubbish idea. Or is it?

The aim is to refine your idea so that it will resonate with the audience. But what if your idea is a bit shit? What if it isn't even your idea? Maybe you've been asked to give the talk. That happens a lot and it's up to you to push back a little and challenge the need to give the talk. Either that or change the talk, make it yours.

This happened to me once. I was asked to give a talk by my dad. He was running a company that tracked traffic flows and turned it into predictive data (think Citymapper decades earlier). Anyway, I read the presentation. It was good but I couldn't see a human angle ... I couldn't see any Velcro. So I added some. I retold the story of when my son was born. Our second child. Our planned home birth all went a bit wrong and we were rushed to hospital in Bradford. At one point I looked out of the windscreen to see us going the wrong way. Into the traffic jam on Manningham Lane. That is not the way to the hospital. I asked the driver what he was doing. Apparently he was a stand-in and didn't know the way. We got caught up in predictable traffic and held up by lights. I told this story. I asked them to imagine how much better it would be if the ambulance was equipped with predictive GPS and Bluetooth identification to change the traffic lights as it approached (all these things are normal now but weren't 25 years ago). This allowed me to bring something quite dry to life. People remember stories, so add some.

Ideas really matter. They will elevate your presentations, they will enhance your communication generally, they are the difference between promotion and not, between that new job and the one you are in. They are the difference between a better world and where we are now.

Remember, the idea is the main thing. But you can help it catch fire with stories.

And that's what we're looking at next.

5
HOW TO TELL STORIES

The best talks tell stories. You know this. Stories fire the imagination. Stories can take your breath away. Stories lift you higher or bring you down.

Using stories I can make you think twice about buying that new iPhone. I can make you cry when I tell you about the boys who dig the coltan from the ground to make the tantalum that makes the capacitors that make the phone work. I can do that with words. Words that put images in your head. Words matter. Stories matter. Furthermore, stories are easier to remember. Not just for you, also for the audience. If you want them to remember your talk then tell them a story.

I'm not saying that you should forget facts. Not at all. Facts are like the raisins in a cake. But it's the story that holds the raisins together. The story is the cake. A piece of cake or a handful of raisins? I'll take the cake.

So how do we take an idea and turn it into a story? According to Christopher Booker in his book, *The Seven Basic Plots*, there are only seven archetypal plot lines in storytelling (rags to riches, the quest, overcoming the monster, and so on). When I teach people to present, I use six main approaches to telling stories. But I'm also cool with them picking an approach of their own. The truth is that it really doesn't matter which approach you follow. They are there to inspire you to tell a better story.

MY 6 FAVOURITE APPROACHES TO STORYTELLING

1. THE HERO'S JOURNEY

This is a traditional storytelling technique. It is linear and takes the audience on a journey. Usually a personal one. Your big idea is still 'the' main thing, but you use your story to illustrate it.

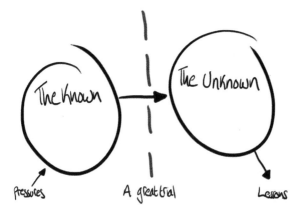

This approach involves moving from the known, the comfortable, the certain, into the unknown. This usually means building tension by talking about the successes and joy of the old situation. So the beginning of the presentation is spent setting up the story. You know the kind of thing. You see it every day in hospital dramas, but this can be done a little clumsily. The joy of kids playing on swings is an inevitable precursor to tragedy. So, my advice is to go gentle with this stuff.

Every hero's journey involves some kind of trial. This is a personal crisis, a realisation that you've climbed the wrong mountain or travelled the wrong path, a business collapse or possibly just a change of heart. But it is likely to involve some kind of trial/difficulty/pivot. This is good. This creates Velcro, a stickiness that will bring people with you.

You could describe the safe space you are in. Maybe the frustration that safety brings. Then the glittering prize or possible brave new world. Then the journey's ups and downs until you arrive at your destination. It kind of doesn't matter if you succeed or not. It's the lessons that matter.

That said, everyone loves a happy ending. Head to the website and watch Rohan Anderson's talk.

2. ORBITING STORIES

In this approach you introduce a central theme. It can be very gently done, very light-touch. Then you support that theme with stories. I see it as a tree with buttress roots. The roots are doing most of the work. The magic is in the supporting stories, but each adds to your central theme.

The structure of the talk can be very loose, and this works really well for those speakers who have a relaxed style. It feels like a series of conversations and then at the end the skill is in pulling all the individual strands together. This approach allows the speaker to roam across a wide range of topics that feel fresh and different but build in a unifying way.

The supporting stories all share the central theme but that is all, they can be very wide ranging in terms of subject and style. It's okay to tell someone else's story as a supporting story, but — obviously — credit them. Each story will build to support the main theme, to lift it a little higher.

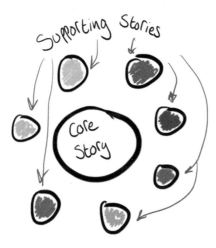

One lovely example of this is from the Do Lectures in 2010. It is a talk from my friend Steve Edge, who we met earlier. Steve is one of the most vibrant people I know. He is a natural storyteller and this approach really suits his natural style. He mentions his central theme almost immediately by responding to something the compere says: 'I guess my talk is more can, than can't'. But if you weren't listening carefully you might miss it. He then goes on to deliver a series of anecdotes that build this theme, including his famous 'Dress for a party every day — and the party will come to you' story.

Now, Steve is an entertaining speaker and he is not technically perfect. And that is just perfect because he is utterly himself and that is all you can be. You can't be me, I can't be you, and neither of us can be Steve Edge.

So those of you who are worried about technical perfection, forgetting your words, losing your flow, stuttering, or any other manner of inconsistency; worry not. It is way less important than you think it is. Give his talk a watch.

3. THE GOLDEN THREAD

The golden thread runs through a presentation. It pops up at different points rather than being visible all the time. I think of it like the raspberry running through raspberry-ripple ice cream.

It could be confused with Orbiting Stories but it's much more like a comedian's call-back. The way this is done is by introducing an idea upfront, then building a presentation that is more linear than Orbiting Stories. At each sub-story you are referring back consciously to the core idea. Use a key phrase to do this.

So you could start with an anecdote that has merit but doesn't seem over-heavy. Then every other story you tell has a strand of that first anecdote in it. Then at the end you resurrect the initial reference again and this makes you look really smart, but also beautifully ends the presentation with an echo of the start. At this point it also gently lifts the other references that you've built into the talk.

When I spoke about my presentations at the end of Chapter 3 I referred to the one that starts with my story about taking the school out on strike when I was nine or ten. I did this because I wanted the freedom to bring sandwiches for lunch rather than have school dinners. We marched up and down the playground until we won and were allowed to bring sandwiches if we wanted to. The problem was my mum wouldn't let me. I had to stick with dinners. On day one of the new regime I was at the front of the queue and facing the nicest of dinner ladies, Mrs Thomas. She looked at me and said, 'I'm glad you're still with us, Mark.' (She knew it was my fault, everyone did!) Then she asked, 'Do you know what would happen if everyone brought sandwiches?'

'No,' I replied.

'I wouldn't have a job, Mark.'

Clang. That was my jaw hitting the floor.

I just hadn't appreciated the implications of what I was doing. It was just a fun thing, a little light disruption. But I learned a big lesson.

WITH POWER COMES RESPONSIBILITY.

This lesson stayed with me. During my talk, that you can find on the accompanying website, I use this line maybe four times. As an aside, as a main reference, almost under my breath sometimes. I then end with a statement that the audience have superpowers and need to use them wisely because (you know it's coming), as that little boy realised all those years ago, with power comes responsibility.

4. OSCILLATION

This approach to storytelling is all about contrast. You build a story structure that highlights the contrast between where we are now, and where we could be; what products and services are like now, and what they could be; how successful our business is now, and how successful it could be; how the culture of our organisation is now, and how it could be.

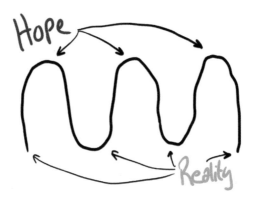

These extremes serve to accentuate the need to change things. You are telling a series of stories that show the future or demonstrate a better way built around your idea. You intersperse these stories with those of the current reality. It is the contrast that captures the imagination. That fires the soul.

You start with either the reality or the better way, then contrast it. You continue this to build a shared vision of the future.

The best example of this is Dr Martin Luther King's 'I have a dream' speech. Actually, this speech is a masterclass in repetition, poetry and pace. We think we all know it, but we don't. Go and watch it again. This talk nearly never happened. Martin had been advised to deliver another talk, that people were bored of his dream one. After starting an alternative talk, it was clear the audience weren't moved. One of congregation shouted, 'Tell them about the dream.' So he did. Even the best presenters need a hand sometimes. See one of the world's most famous talks at: *dopresent.co.uk/talks*

This can be used to sell washing-up liquid — imagine a world where your dishes weren't just clean, they were eco-clean. It can seem a little trite or shallow, but oscillation draws attention to the upside by placing it next to the downside.

5. IN AT THE DEEP END

This requires courage. It also requires a great story. There are no frills with this one. The audience is thrown straight in at the deep end. Now this doesn't mean that the first sentence has to be dramatic. You can still spend a minute or two in the set-up.

You start with a big hook that somewhere, within the first minute or two, you drop straight into the heart of the story.

The key is surprise; however, it can still be gently done. The challenge with this approach is the need to deliver. It is a brave approach and your story and style need to match that.

One example that does this perfectly is a talk by Zak Ebrahim. He doesn't drop the surprise in straight away. He actually builds a little tension first. It would be easy for him to start with 'I'm the son of a terrorist'. But he doesn't. He sets the scene. He builds a picture. He describes the terrorist actions of El Sayyid Nosair: the loss of life, the disruption, the imprisonment. Then he drops the line: 'El Sayyid Nosair is my father.' You're hooked. All the questions are running around your head: Did he just say that? How does he feel? What was it like growing up with a terrorist? You're 'in' and you don't want to get out.

Whether he intended it or not there is an added dimension. Anyone with a basic knowledge of *Star Wars* will feel the echo of Darth Vader in those words. This cultural reference is a genius stroke as it wraps up all the themes of those first (to be made) three films and passes the parcel to the watcher. The talk is brilliant, well worth a watch.

6. A FALSE START

This approach is based on the audience expectation that the presentation will go in a certain direction. But the presenter takes it in an entirely different one. Often the lessons are not evident until the end. It requires a little patience from the audience but it can be really powerful. It can, sometimes, feel a little like the Hero's Journey.

I've chosen J.K. Rowling as my example. Not only does she deliver a brilliant talk, she sets her unexpected start out really clearly at the beginning. She is delivering a commencement speech at Harvard University. On a day where most speakers would be expected to talk about success and real life, she opts to extol the virtues of failure and imagination.

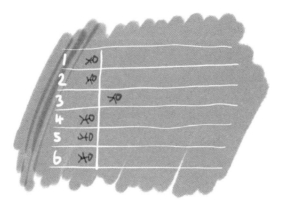

The structure and pace of the talk is (as you'd expect) near-genius. She is also very funny and delivers some killer one-liners. The talk is one of my favourites. Watch it for yourself on the website.

You may prefer, of course, to ignore all of these storytelling approaches and go your own way. That is perfectly fine. I have included them so you have a possible structure or framework that you can build a story around. Structure and form are as important as content, because they give confidence and shape to a talk.

STRUCTURING AND PLANNING YOUR STORY

Having an idea, having an approach to a story, is a great start but it really helps me when I'm able to plan my presentations out. I draw them out in chunks. Maybe six chunks. I use a picture for each chunk — like a storyboard. But you could just use words.

You may have used storyboarding in your job. If so, then that really helps. I've added a couple of templates to the back of the book. Fill them in as you see fit. Bear in mind that you will need to *remember* the storyboard, so simple wins for me. I break my talk down into an intro, four stories and an ending. The stories I have are my own personal stories. They are irrefutable. I won't forget them because they happened to me. I then hang facts, points or arguments off those stories. Or, perhaps more accurately, I bring facts, points and arguments *to life* with those stories. I use pictures, but feel free to use words.

To further help you plan your approach, you can download a simple PDF workbook from *dopresent.co.uk/ resources*.

6
YOUR AUDIENCE

Knowing your audience is essential. Not just in formal presentations, but when trying to communicate any idea. It's important to know who you are talking to, what they already know, what they expect, what they don't expect, and how you want them to feel, and what you want them to think, afterwards.

The aim of any talk, indeed any communication, is to make the audience feel differently about something or feel more deeply about something. This will then lead to the audience doing something differently, changing a behaviour, buying something off you, believing in your brand over another. While we don't start at the end, we do start with the end in mind. Defining the output of the talk before you write it is a great way of building structure. Understanding what you want the audience to do afterwards will help develop a talk that moves people. I always start with AA: Audience Afterwards.

The only time I fell flat on my face with a presentation was when I forgot to consider the audience. I had been delivering talks on the environmental impact of electrical waste. I had been doing this to the manufacturing industry and I'd developed a talk and a style that fitted that audience.

The presentation included a slide that was a screen-grab from the Greenpeace website. It was a picture of a sex toy with the words: 'How green is your sex toy?' It wasn't offensive. Well, it hadn't been to my normal audience, but it was to the audience of business professionals at their annual conference in London. It went down *really* badly. I had failed to adapt my talk for the audience. A cardinal error. I could feel them slipping away from me, detaching from me and therefore my presentation.

Once they've turned off you aren't going to easily get them back. And so it proved. It was a watershed moment for how and what I presented. It was a minor thing, with important lessons. People were really offended. The image didn't belong to me, but *I* chose to show it. I sat on the train on the way home and rewrote four presentations. And I never used that slide again.

UNDERSTANDING THE AUDIENCE

Understanding what the audience want, what they expect and who they are is vital to tailoring your presentation, your story. It's likely that the message, the meaning and the value of your talk will remain the same. But the way you deliver it and the styles you use will change.

Put yourself in the position of the audience. Why are they at this event, this pitch, this briefing? What are they hoping to gain from it? Why have they given up their time to sit and listen to you? What are they hoping to learn? How can you surpass their expectations? What do you want them to think afterwards? How do you want them to feel? What do you want them to do?

The first step in this is to find out who will be there. Ask the organisers of the event or meeting. If it's a big event the organisers will have developed a marketing strategy and targeted specific sectors. Talk to them and find out who they've targeted. They will have an attendance list, and perhaps a list of job titles associated with bookings. This is a good way to begin to build a picture of the audience. Ask for it. Take another look at the blurb they sent out. What is the tone of the event? How about the language that they use?

Now, please don't try to mirror this. Don't try and fit in. It's important to stand out, but to do so with knowledge of the audience's expectations and how far you can push your talk. Your aim is to exceed expectations without missing the audience's aspirations.

It is also really important to take a look at the other speakers or people presenting. Who are they? What will they be talking about? What is their style? We live in an age where you can probably find footage of the other speakers online. Take a look. What is their audience engagement like? Furthermore, take a look at any footage from previous events (if this is an event) and, if you know any of the previous speakers, then give them a call and ask how the audience were.

GET TO KNOW THE SPACE

It is also important to understand the space that you will be in. I had a period of presenting in large exhibition spaces. You could attract a big old audience, but those spaces leak sound like a colander passes water. It's harder to engage an audience in a big space. You may need to be a bigger version of you. Conversely, a smaller and more intimate space may not be suited to running around like a six-year-old. Find out about the space and get there early (before the event starts) so you can get a measure of it.

GET THERE EARLY

Arriving early is important. It's important to see the speakers before you, or at least the speaker immediately before you. This will give you a good idea of the level of audience engagement and audience expectation. It also grounds you in the culture of the event. It avoids any style shocks.

Here's an example of style shock. I'm lucky to be one of the Founding Partners of the Do Lectures. That isn't a Founder. The event was founded by David and Clare Hieatt, but during the event's early years a few like-minded individuals came on board to offer support. I'm one of those. Anyway, a few years ago we had a speaker who arrived half an hour before his slot. For those of you that haven't been to the lectures, the culture of the event is very laid-back and very modest. This speaker hadn't been before, hadn't done any research and started his talk by saying how he'd flown in on a private jet from St Tropez. No one was impressed. It's not that kind of event. He then stood in the middle of the stage, arms outstretched, and declared, 'I'm sixty-three, do you still fancy me?' Again, it went down really badly. He had completely failed to understand the audience, their expectations and aspirations. It was a long way back from that point. Arguably, he didn't win us back.

So, get to the event early, understand the event, get a feel for the audience. Don't blend in completely but be sensitive to the audience's aspirations and needs. Be human and be modest. (But beware of fake modesty. The audience will sniff it out.)

Being human, being vulnerable, are both covered in a later chapter. They are great ways of engaging the audience, and audience engagement really matters. But remember, not everyone in the audience will like you, will want to hear what you are saying, or even believe you. Your job is not to make friends or to be liked. Your job is to spread ideas, spread new thinking, and shift their thinking. As my friend (and this book's cover designer) James Victore says:

"YOU ARE NOT FOR EVERYONE, JUST THE SEXY PEOPLE."

I spent a long time thinking a successful talk was one when the audience wanted to be my friend. It's nice when they do, but focus on the change you want to make in their lives and/or work first.

If you're delivering a pitch or briefing the same applies. Understanding who is in the room is vital to the success of the pitch. Sure, their job functions are important, but so too are their hobbies, their likes and dislikes. It sounds a bit stalkery, but if this is a big pitch then take a look at their social media, their LinkedIn. What are they saying and what are they doing? How can you use words, imagination and story to help them relate to, and connect with, you?

It is also really important to be adaptable. I once gave a talk on environmental issues at the Mother and Baby show (yep, I'm guessing it's called the Parent and Baby show now). I'd written a twenty-minute piece about chemical safety in bottles, teats and toys. I had to do it three times across the day. The first one was great. I had maybe fifty people in the audience. All good. The second went even better, maybe a hundred people. But the last ... one person turned up. Now, at this stage it would have been foolish to stand on a platform and deliver a 'talk' (although I have seen that done), so I sat in the audience with the only person there and we talked for the twenty minutes about their specific situation. They got way more out of it than they would a normal presentation (and I didn't feel daft).

AUDIENCE CHECKLIST

I have pulled together a checklist of ways to ensure you understand your audience:

1. **Who are the audience?** What sectors are they from? What are their broad interests?

2. **What will they be expecting?** What have they been exposed to at this event already? What are the big themes apparent in their industry, in the broader sector, in society? How does your talk or pitch relate to, build on or remedy these things?

3. **What do they believe in?** This is clearly a tricky question and you will have no way of really knowing. But you'll be able to pick up an idea by being there early, from speaking to people at the coffee break. Keep your radar on. Try and determine what their beliefs and values align with.

4. **What story is likely to bring you both together?** What can you include in your talk or your pitch that is unifying? There is a time for being challenging, but it is not when trying to build engagement. I use music. I use purpose. I make my beliefs clear by using stories from my past. These stories are mine but they can unify. As James Joyce said: 'In the particular is contained the universal.'

5. **What do you want them to feel?** What feelings do you want them to have afterwards? This can be really broad. Feelings like hope, positivity, ambition, self-improvement, love. It sounds a bit hippy, but write down those feelings you want to encourage.

6. **What do you want them to think as they stand up to leave?** How do you want to have shifted their thinking? Do you want them to be kinder, to value innovation more, to think about the sustainability (in all ways) of their business models? Write down how you want them to think differently.

7. **What do you want them to do when they get back to work, their project, or home?** Now don't be disappointed if they don't email you the following day and tell you all the changes they've made to themselves or their organisation, but dare to dream big. What is it you'd really like them to do? What behaviour would you like them to change? What habits need to be formed to change that behaviour? And finally, and hardest of all, what beliefs do you need to change to make that happen? Sharpen that pencil and get them down.

8. **What can you include in your presentation to make all this easier?** Stories, media, examples. What's in your arsenal?

Understanding your audience is key. You wouldn't launch a new product without understanding the market, without undertaking research, without aligning your product with their beliefs. So don't do it with your presentation.

7
CONFIDENCE

This is it. This is the hummus in the sandwich. This is the main thing. Confidence is attractive. It is even 'sexy'. Getting closer to the real 'you' means you can stop projecting the fake one.

This chapter looks at confidence. It looks at why people struggle with confidence. How it varies from situation to situation. It examines and helps define limiting beliefs. It looks at who put them there. Why? How they can be inherited. How they are comfortable (like a pair of slippers), but how this doesn't serve anyone (like worn-out slippers). It looks at how to remove them. It then moves on to outline a number of simple approaches to boosting confidence, to dealing with the dry rot that erodes confidence.

Confidence is the key to a great talk. Confidence is not charisma (I can help teach confidence, but charisma is harder — it's more innate). Confidence is not ego (being good at something and knowing it is not having an ego; being average or poor at something and thinking you're great — that's ego). Confidence is not showing off — confidence is showing up, and showing up with belief in yourself and an understanding of your weaknesses as well as your strengths. It isn't bluffing or blagging or hustling. It is being utterly certain who you are.

Confidence is really complex. Some people seem to be born confident. There is interesting research suggesting that confidence is genetic — as much as 50 per cent of our likelihood of being confident is thought to be genetic. Some develop confidence (that'll be the other 50 per cent, then). Some have confidence knocked out of them (sometimes through love as much as hate) as they grow. But the good news is that there are many simple things you can do to improve confidence.

First, I want you to consider what confidence is. It isn't a fixed attribute. Sometimes we'll have more or less confidence in the same situation than at other times. Sometimes our confidence is dented by things that don't relate to the task in hand. Sometimes our confidence is bolstered (or undermined) by the clothes we choose to wear for an event (this is bordering on ceremony and ritual here, but more of that later).

Confidence is the outcome of the thoughts we have, the actions we take and how we feel about ourselves. Sure, these can all be affected by others, by external situations, by the journey to the event — or to this part of our lives. And fortunately, some of it can be rectified.

LIMITING BELIEFS

Before we get into the tips and tricks, the strategies and approaches, I want to talk about limiting beliefs. As mentioned previously, one of the things that holds us back in terms of confidence (and in so many other ways too) is our limiting beliefs. What is a limiting belief? It is a view of ourselves that keeps us small, that limits the person that we could be. It is a set view of ourselves that tightly defines us, that holds us down. This view has become normalised to the point that we can't even see the constraints on our own thinking. We have had these constraints for so long that they have become invisible. It's a bit like carrying around a big rucksack of pebbles. You become so used to the weight of the rucksack that you only notice the weight when you take the rucksack off. The rucksack has become part of you. It's the same with limiting beliefs, or fears. You only realise how constraining they were once they've gone. So how do we get rid of them?

There is a legendary experiment conducted by Karl Mobius, a German zoologist, in 1873 that demonstrates this beautifully. In the experiment Mobius placed a pike (a large carnivorous fish) in a big tank of water. Into the tank Mobius released a few smaller fish. As the pike was carnivorous, it ate the smaller fish. Mobius then lowered a large glass bell jar that was open at the bottom and the top into the tank. The pike was on the outside of the bell jar. Inside the jar Mobius placed more small fish. The pike could see the fish but not the glass bell jar. *Eh up*, it thought, *dinner*. It charged at the smaller fish and all it got in return was a sore nose. It tried to eat the smaller fish numerous times and just got more and more hurt and increasingly depressed. Finally, it seemed to give up. It sank to the bottom of the tank and looked glum. Mobius then lifted the bell jar out. There was now nothing between the pike and the smaller fish. Yet the pike stayed at the bottom of the tank. The smaller fish were free and swam all over the tank. Over the top of the pike, down its side and across its nose. Still the pike didn't budge. It didn't try and eat the smaller fish. Its limiting belief was that it couldn't. So it didn't even try.

Others repeated this experiment, in the days before animal cruelty was a thing. What do you think happened to the pike? Yep, that's right. It starved to death. Starved to death surrounded by food. We go bust surrounded by great business opportunities. We struggle to find the right people surrounded by the best talent in the world. We can't make ourselves heard but have every word at our beck and call. We run out of ideas surrounded by all the stimulus you could shake a stick at. Our limiting beliefs keep us where we are. We can't grow as a business because we don't do that 'thing', recruit those people, aren't brave enough to talk to those potential clients, deliver that presentation. We don't grow as people because our comfort zone is too damn comfortable. Because we can't express our ideas, our desires, our views, ourselves — we stay small. We stay safe. These are limiting beliefs and while they may have helped you in the past, may have helped you stay safe, they now hold you back. Time to thank them, and discard them.

It is really common to pick up a few limiting beliefs as we go through life. Some of those are given to us by our parents (mostly to keep us safe, occasionally to ensure we don't make them feel like they weren't 'enough'); sometimes by our colleagues or bosses at work (this is nearly always a result of them not wanting to be out-performed by you, or their desire to control you; I've seen this often in my thirty years in business, even in those who, allegedly, specialise in building teams — all driven by fear).

It is also really common for someone to steal your voice. They do this by intimating that what you say isn't important. This could simply be by not listening to you or it could be more strongly expressed. Rubbishing what people say is really common both at work and at home. No one has the right to silence you. Your words matter and they deserve to be heard. In my workshops I see this again and again, and sadly it is more common that women have their words stolen by men, than the other way around.

Now, this limiting belief stuff is complex. To demonstrate, I want to talk to you about fleas. Yep, fleas. To train fleas for a flea circus (yes, they do still exist) you need to restrict the height that they can jump. Fleas are amazing jumpers and can jump up to 60cm high. Now, in flea circuses you may only want them to jump 20cm. How do you train them to do that? You place them in a jar that is 20cm tall, and pop a lid on the jar. And leave them there for three days. After this time you can take the lid off and they won't jump out. You can tip them out of the jar and they will only jump 20cm. There's no jar but they won't jump higher than 20cm. Fascinating, right? Not the most fascinating part of the story. When those fleas reproduce and lay eggs, when those eggs hatch and turn into larvae and eventually into adult fleas, how high do you think they will jump? Yep, 20cm and no higher.

Fleas inherit the limiting beliefs of their parents and so do we. You may be scared of money because your parents are, you may fear social interaction because your parents do, you may keep yourself small because your parents did the same, you may fear being seen or heard because your parents did. As J.K. Rowling says in her Harvard Commencement speech:

"THERE IS A SELL-BY DATE ON BLAMING YOUR PARENTS."

Thank your parents for keeping you safe, then ditch those constraints and become the person you always wanted to be. This is bigger than presenting.

Your limiting beliefs have kept you in your comfort zone and they've done that really successfully, but they don't serve you any more. It's time to move on.

HOW TO BE MORE CONFIDENT

So how do we improve our confidence? How do we become more confident when presenting?

I have a number of suggestions to help you.

1. SPEND MORE TIME WITH YOURSELF

We don't get bored any more. We don't sit with our own discomfort any more. When was the last time you were on your own without your phone? You're never alone with a phone. The single best way to improve confidence is to work out who you are. And, trust me, it's better to do this earlier rather than later in life. What do I mean by this? You need to learn to like yourself, to know yourself, to love yourself. To be able to look in the mirror and like the person you see is what I'm talking about. We need to spend time with ourselves to get to this point. I don't mind how you do this. Gardening, running, swimming, walking, meditating, I really don't care — but spending time alone and undistracted is the key.

2. GO THROUGH ANY POSSIBLE QUESTIONS

One of the biggest fears we have around presenting relates to difficult questions. Questions we can't answer. There are two strategies to deal with this. Firstly, find that really difficult person in your office / studio / friendship group / family. Tell them about your presentation (the idea and story) and ask them what questions they would ask. They are programmed to look for the challenge. This is a skill, so use them for it.

Secondly, be honest. If someone asks a question that you can't answer then just be honest: 'That's a great question,

I don't know the answer but I'll find out.' But remember to get back to them.

Occasionally during a presentation you will encounter someone who just doesn't like you, who wants to trip you up. This is a challenge and the best strategy is to neutralise them. 'Hey, it's unlikely that we will agree on this but why don't we talk about it afterwards?' The audience will undoubtedly back you. You can argue with this person later (if need be) and get on and deliver the talk. I had this recently. It related to the unsustainability of a glass package wrapped in plastic. I was challenged. I acknowledged the point of view but repeated the fact that it wasn't the best environmental option. I was challenged again, then again. So I just said, 'I don't agree and it is unlikely that we will reach consensus; let's talk afterwards.' It spared the audience the debate and let me get on with the rest of the presentation.

3. BE THANKFUL THAT YOU'VE BEEN GIVEN THIS OPPORTUNITY

Not everyone gets asked to do this. Just you. That means you are valued and trusted, that means someone thinks you have an interesting point of view and fresh ideas. So don't disappoint, don't play safe. It's time to stand up and show up. For many, being in front of an audience is being out of control. Flip it. Being in front of an audience is being in total control. I can make you think of a pink balloon just by saying the words. I can make you laugh, I can make you cry. Being in front of people is like being a DJ with ideas and emotions. When we panic, when we have a wobble, it is tempting to reach for the brakes. But as anyone who rides mountain bikes will tell you, speed is your friend: power through.

4. REHEARSE

But not too much. I hate rehearsing. It removes my spontaneity, my relaxed delivery. But I acknowledge that the presentation is better on the tenth outing than on the first. I have a friend. He rehearses a lot. He once rehearsed 26 times for a presentation to a big UK retailer. Afterwards they said it was the best presentation they'd ever seen. Now he rehearses 26 times for everything. So this has moved from rehearsal to ritual. Like putting your left boot on first before a big match. Multiple rehearsals work for his talks, regardless of *why* it works for him. Personally I don't rehearse, and neither does Brené Brown. Find out what level of rehearsal works for you. Then stick to that.

5. BE AWARE OF YOUR LIMITING BELIEFS

Know what they are. Be comfortable that they are part of you. Put them in their place. Their place is not in your head or on this stage now.

6. CHECK YOUR DECK

This sounds simplistic but it is really important. Ensure you know the order, ensure the spelling and grammar are correct, ensure that it's the correct deck. It sounds daft, but I once started a presentation to a recycling forum with a deck I'd been writing on the train for a heating ventilation and air conditioning forum (I'm so bloody niche!) It was embarrassing to say the least — there's no easy way out of that one. You just have to admit your mistake and flick it over to the correct deck.

If you're using your laptop also be aware of what other windows are left open. Mail notifications popping up top-

right are distracting. And be aware of what else is visible.
I once saw a great talk on blockchain that started with the
presenter connecting her laptop and revealing her bank
balance. It wasn't healthy. It put her off, reduced audience
confidence, and ruined what would have been a great talk.
So shut everything down apart from your deck. The last
thing you want to be worrying about is the tech or your
slides. Get there early enough to ensure it all works.

7. DON'T FORGET TO BREATHE

All that is great, but you're still shaking like a leaf, right?
Absolutely pooping yourself? This is panic. Panic is
debilitating. Panic can end in hyperventilation and the
inability to be able to think clearly or speak coherently.
Panic is not your friend. Having a few nerves, well, that's
okay. Indeed, being a little nervous is good. I deliver my
worst presentations when I'm *not* nervous. The most
nervous I get is before the auction at the Do Lectures.
The auction is when we raise money for good causes by
selling experiences with the speakers. It could be climbing
Kilimanjaro with Charlie Engle, or making your own batch
of alcohol-free gin with Seedlip founder Ben Branson.
In short, things money can't normally buy. Why do I get
nervous? Because it really matters. Because the money
we raise is donated to charity and people might live or
die as a result. It's an auction, but I structure it like a
performance. It has inspiration at the front end, some
self-deprecation, running themes (golden threads),
humour, and a big ending. I use audience participation,
I will hustle occasionally. It is utterly exhausting and I have
to consciously remember to breathe — but that's what gets
me through.

MANAGING NERVES

Breathing is one of three things I do to manage nerves. The breathing technique that follows is called alternate nostril breathing. It's a simple process that serves to slow the breathing down to five breaths a minute. Five to six breaths a minute has been clinically shown to reduce anxiety, increase relaxation and increase Heart Rate Variability (keep your eye on HRV — it is fast becoming an indicator of cardiovascular health, stress loading and overall wellbeing). This is how it's done:

1. Sit in a comfortable position

2. Place your left hand on your lap

3. Lift your right hand to your nose and exhale completely

4. Use your right thumb to close your right nostril

5. Inhale through your left nostril for a count of eight and then close the left nostril with one of your fingers

6. Open the right nostril and exhale through this side for a count of four

7. Inhale through the right nostril for a count of eight and then close this nostril

8. Open the left nostril and exhale through the left side for a count of four

9. Repeat from step four

10. Continue for up to five minutes

Breathing is a big part of presentations, as it is in singing. Try not to snatch breath, try not to over-breathe. Over-breathing is common. Taking too much oxygen in and too often becomes addictive. Slow it all down. Try and breathe through your nose all the time. Even during light exercise. A classic sign of over-breathing is mouth-breathing. If you're a mouth-breather you most likely over-breathe, and over-breathing results in rushed breathing when talking and a more nasal tone. You'll know if you're a mouth-breather as you will dribble while sleeping. There are many health and physical exercise benefits of nose-breathing and they are covered in Patrick McKeown's book *The Oxygen Advantage*, along with a series of exercises designed to correct this.

Nervousness and panic clutter the mind. The secret is to see it and recognise it but see *beyond* it. The second technique I use is a simple meditation technique. It is called RAIN and you will find it explained on a number of websites. But here is my simple explanation.

RECOGNISING

Recognise what is happening in your mind: anxiety; fear; stress. Identify it. For example, this is Fear, I recognise you. Where do I feel it in my body? Tight chest; tension; heart rate. Recognise it and give it a name. Hello Fear, my old friend.

ALLOWING

Don't push it away. Don't criticise yourself for feeling this way. Why add a second layer when you're already feeling shit? It gives the feeling more power. Whatever you feel is okay. Allow yourself to feel the emotions and physical stuff. Don't add any more judgement on top.

INVESTIGATING

Give the experience the kindness of your attention. What is calling for attention? What is dominant? Notice it and accept it without pushing it away. How does your body feel right now? Where is the tension or movement? Are the sensations changing? Investigate how you are seeing things. Can you allow what is happening or are you looking through a filter or lens? What opinions are you placing on the situation?

NON-IDENTIFYING

It's best not to see this feeling as 100 per cent part of yourself. You are bigger than it. Observe it with balance, but don't identify with it. Relax the mind and think of the sky / cloud metaphor. The sky doesn't change as the clouds pass by. The sky is not the weather. It is the sky. Your mind is bigger and detached from the things it is thinking now.

This can all feel a little worthy, a bit hippy. But I'm a really big fan of meditation. It brings calm and it brings perspective.

The third thing I do before I go on stage is a little Qigong centering. Now, I'm acutely aware that this can make me look ridiculous—like someone bringing in an aeroplane to land. But it works for me. Like my mate's 26 rehearsals, it has probably moved into ritual now. I don't mind. I still do it. This is what I do: I stand straight. I place both arms straight down and palm up. So, they are at six o'clock. I then breathe in for a count of eight, and slowly raise my right arm in a circular motion to the right. At eight seconds it will be at twelve o'clock and I then count to four as I bring it down the front of my body to join the left hand. I then repeat the process on the other side with my left hand. I do this for four or six cycles. Yes, I look daft; no, I don't care.

The observant among you will notice that the timing of the breathing (eight seconds in and four out) is the same as that used in alternate nostril breathing. Like that exercise, centering is a way of calming the breath and therefore the heart, and hopefully the mind. As I say, it has become a form of ritual for me too.

Calming panic, reducing nerves, easing the breath, all help prepare you to open your mouth and speak. Actually, they prepare you to do anything that makes you uncomfortable. So don't fight your breath. Work with it.

8
TECHNIQUE

I can't be you, and you can't be me. I can't be Steve Jobs, and you can't be Brené Brown. All we can be is ourselves. And that's enough.

It's important to remember that while presentations are performances, they aren't acts. You are not being someone else up there, you are being the best version of you, a bigger version of you. More of this later.

The secret is to understand what makes you unique, to find those foibles and idiosyncrasies. The things that made you odd as a kid, the things you tried to stop doing when you became a teenager; those things are what we are looking for now. You need to understand those things and use them to your advantage. They are your presentation personality, your fingerprint. They are your friend.

If you're lively and energetic then make a thing out of that. Watching Gavin Strange at the Do Lectures you can't fail to observe his high level of energy as he runs around the stage. Engaging and compelling, it is a perfect style for Gavin. Seeing Louisa Thomsen Brits present, however, was a serene experience. She walked onto the stage with a silent grace. Sat down cross-legged, leaned forward and spoke gently. The roof of the building dropped lower to meet her, and we all leaned in towards her. We all listened harder in response to her style. Tim Smit, on the other hand, gave a talk at the Do Lectures that was liquid and relaxed. It was like being in a conversation with him. It was brilliant and made you feel very close to him. All three had massively different styles and all three worked a treat.

The most you can do is remember yourself on a good day; no, a great day. We've all had those conversations where we shone, where people wanted to hear more from us, where the words flowed freely and we built images with them. That's what we are trying to channel, that's the performance we need: to be in our element. To get you in *your* element you need to try less hard; try less hard to be something you are not.

There are a number of things to consider when thinking about technique. There are no hard rules, there is nothing you shouldn't do. All those 'golden rules' that have dogged presentation-skills training since the creation of PowerPoint can be forgotten. And yes, I'll cover PowerPoint too. In fact, let's dive into that first.

SLIDE ETIQUETTE

The phrase 'Death by PowerPoint' is unfair. PowerPoint doesn't kill people, presenters do (with apologies to Goldie Looking Chain). But we all know what people mean when they say it. I'm lucky (I think) in that I started presenting in the age of colour-positive slide transparencies. Presenters would bring their own carousel of slides with them and the presentation was punctuated with the 'ker-ching, click' of the mechanism. Plus the audience had to sit in the dark to ensure the projection could be seen. Slides were often upside down and back to front. It was a nightmare. Then along came overhead projectors. You would use a word-processing package to write content and then print onto a plastic sheet that went on the projector. Because there were no transitions and no builds you would need to cover the slide up with a piece of paper and slowly move the paper down as you presented. Furthermore, images were just dreadful and best avoided. Horrible. Then PowerPoint arrived.

It was a revelation. Images worked. They helped build tension and stories. But the transitions ... well, they were dreadful. Words came flying in, heralded by sounds. It was anarchy and all it did was serve to distract from the message. And that's my main point about slides. They are there for two reasons and the first of those is to add emphasis, depth or emotion to your story. The second is to retain a structure.

So, your slides must add something to your presentation but they must not get in the way. My top tips for slides include doing a section of your talk without any. Yep, that's right. It's good to click the magic button on the remote that turns the screen to black (or insert a black slide into the deck), put the clicker down, come centre stage, and deliver a chunk of the talk without any slides at all. You know your story, you know you can do it, and it looks like you are mega-confident. Even if you need slides, I heartily recommend delivering a section of the talk without any.

But you will inevitably have some slides in each presentation, and these are the things that have worked for me:

1. FONTS

Keep it simple. I love Helvetica. It is a sans serif font and is quite tight but allows easy differentiation between a, e and o. Which really helps those with dyslexia. Other sans serif fonts are also ace, including Gill Sans. But this is all about personal preference and I'm not going to tell you what to do other than keep it simple.

2. TRANSITIONS

Honestly, I just don't use them. If you do, make sure they are simple and do not distract.

3. NOISE

Keep logos, brand messaging and other slide 'furniture' to a minimum. Templates are your enemy.

4. IMAGES

Images win. One image replaces lots of words. Images are nicer to look at than words. Images are international. Search for Creative Commons images (that you can use without infringing the copyright holder's rights) or use your own images. Advanced searches in most search engines will allow you to search for Creative Commons images.

5. MEDIA

I use media a lot. I use the Nike Walt Stack film to explain purpose; I use a short clip of Simon Sinek to remind people why they matter; I use a film of Derek Redmond in the 1992 Olympics to talk about persistence, brand and parents; I use a film of a Canadian rock band to talk about the third marketing revolution — the end of control; I use an advert for sanitary products to reveal misogyny; I use clips of Martin Luther King and James Baldwin to talk about racism; I use pop music of the 1970s and 1980s to demonstrate literally anything. Media can convey a point that you want to make faster and in a more beautiful way than I can. But only use it if it does so, if it adds something, if it takes your talk to a new level. I've seen it used really badly. I've seen one speaker show four films about his aerial slide company in a talk that wasn't supposed to be a sales pitch. Media isn't there to fill time, to count the minutes. Make the minutes count, and only use media if it lifts your talk.

HOW TO STAND

After slides, the thing I get asked about most just before people go on stage is what to do with their body.

Don't stand behind the lectern. Unless it is the only place with a microphone and the space requires you to use one. Always ask for a cheek or lapel mic, or failing that a handheld. The lectern hides you and this is your moment. Stand in the light that you deserve and be totally seen. Come centre stage and speak from there. Sure, you may need notes, and it's fine to have those on the lectern. You can always walk over to them if you need to. Moving is not a problem. It's okay to wander back to get your notes. The same with a drink.

Stand strong. A good friend and photographer once told me that the way to have a great photograph taken of yourself is to imagine all the people you love, all your success, just behind you. Stand with pride in front of your successes. I use this technique on the stage. In James Kerr's book *Legacy* he talks about one of the initiation processes that the New Zealand All Blacks go through. When they get given their shirt they are told to put it on, then to imagine all the players in that position that came before, all the giants, all the stories and myths. Then they are asked to imagine all the great players that will come after them. They are asked to imagine these players standing in front of them. That's a powerful image right there. Then they are asked to imagine their importance in this line, to feel the pride of being in the line in the first place and feel the sense of power of being in the line and then, of course, the sense of responsibility that brings with it. Successes behind you. Future (opportunity) in front of you. When you take to the stage try and imagine all the success you have had, all the people that love and care for you sat behind you. Willing you on.

MOVING AROUND

There are no rules here. If you are feeling lively move, if not then don't. I move a lot. I pace around the stage and 'act out' scenarios. But I also spend sections completely stationary. I value both and it really depends on your personality and style. Don't run around if that's not you. Don't try and be Gavin Strange if you're quiet, and don't try and be still like Louisa Thomsen Brits if you're prone to bobbing about the stage. Move if you feel like moving and stay still if you don't. We are looking for an enhanced you rather than you trying to be anyone else.

PAUSES AND SILENCES

The spaces between words and sentences are important. In my workshops we start with everyone doing a short talk and there are usually one or two that 'ermmm' between sentences. This isn't because the speaker can't think of an idea or loses the thread of their narrative; it is usually because they don't want to leave a moment of silence. If there's a moment of silence someone may slip in a tricky question, it might look like you've forgotten what's coming next.

Silences show confidence. Silences can be used to add emphasis and drama (but don't overdo it). Don't be afraid of them.

USE THE RIGHT WORDS, NOT ALL THE WORDS.

USING NOTES

Using notes is fine. There is a common misperception that being 'note free' is the holy grail of presentation skills. There is, of course, a level of polish that comes with a presentation without notes. But sometimes we need help remembering stuff. My personal struggle is with statistics, but it can also help to write down a rough structure. Your slides provide a structure of course, but if I'm presenting without slides, at the great OneTrackMinds events, for example, I might have a list of topics written down. There is no detail here, just single words that prompt me. I compare it to navigating in a car in the 1980s, before satnav. If I was driving from my home in Leicester to Swanage (great holiday town) I wouldn't have anything other than a list of towns written down.

It would look like this:

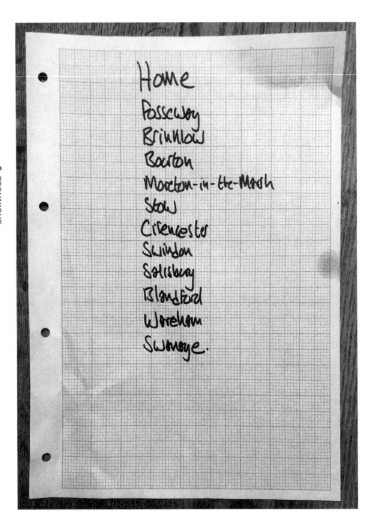

And my OneTrackMinds notes look like this:

You don't need detail. You need shape, you need to have a cue for the next stop, the next story. If you need to know the current atmospheric carbon dioxide concentration level when you're talking about The Smiths (yep, that's what I do sometimes) then write down 348ppm next to it (we are now at 411ppm — not good). Even write notes on the back of your hand if you need to. Do not use your phone. It needs waking up, it shines a ghastly up-light on your face and it looks shite.

LEARNING FROM STAND-UP COMEDIANS

TECHNIQUE

While there are many fantastic talks that you can see on YouTube, on the Do Lectures website and on the TED and TEDx platforms, it is worth casting the net even wider for inspiration.

I'm a big fan of watching videos and listening to podcasts that explain the structure of thinking that sits at the heart of stand-up comedy. I stumbled upon this one night. I suffer a little from insomnia. I drift off okay but often wake around 3 am and can't get back to sleep. Once, in an attempt to occupy the small hours, I googled videos of my favourite comedian (unsurprisingly, this is Stewart Lee). After watching a couple of clips of his stand-up shows, a talk by him explaining about the structure of his art began to auto-play. I was hooked. I sat up in bed, grabbed a pen and made loads of notes. These are some of the things I learnt.

— **You are not playing a role.** You are projecting a bigger version of yourself. You can learn this from comedians but also from the musician David Byrne who, faced with bigger venues, took the advice of one of the finest choreographers ever, Toni Basil. She advised him that to translate his quirky performance from a smaller stage to a bigger one he just needed to wear an oversized suit. His trademark quirkiness became accentuated and he was more visible.

— **Timing is everything.** I mean *everything*. Your presentation is a performance and the slides need to change at the right time, your delivery needs to be timed and you need to be patient with your lines.

— **Nothing happens by accident.** Structure is key, even if you want your talk to feel unstructured.

— **Your jokes should be about you,** about your tribe, not about other people. But remember to avoid too much self-deprecation.

— **Pauses are a sign of strength,** not weakness.

— Finally, please remember that **you are not a comedian;** even if you are funnier than average.

If you want to learn how to hold the room, structure a performance and take the audience with you, take lessons from stand-ups. But also take lessons from singers. Liam Gallagher from Oasis is a case in point. He stands at about 172cm tall (around five foot eight). Not massive. Regardless of the season, he is dressed for winter. He has his microphone way too high so that he has to crane his head up and forward.

But despite this, you can't take your eyes off him. He has a charisma that is undeniable. Even if you don't like Oasis.

In short, there are no wrong techniques. Wear what you want, move naturally, be yourself.

9
ENDING WELL

You know those disappointing songs that just fade out, that take the volume down so gently that you don't notice they've finished? You don't want to end a presentation like that. You need to end positively, and people need to know it is the end.

I went to see one of my heroes perform recently. I was so excited and so wanted to enjoy the evening. I know what a genius he is, I've read his books, I loved his TV show, and I'm a massive fan of his art. But I wasn't so keen on his stage show. There were various reasons, but mostly it lacked structure. So much so that when he finished no one knew he'd finished and he had to say, 'Er, that's the end of the show.' If people don't know you've reached the end, then you've not done it right. This is a short but important chapter on how to finish.

I like to finish with an echo of whatever I started with. Most usually I start with the story of taking the primary school out on strike. The key line in this story is 'with power comes responsibility'. As previously discussed, I'll drop this line in once or twice as I talk. Then at the end I'll say that the work the audience does is powerful. Then use the picture below, which is my recreation of the last panel of Stan Lee's first *Spiderman* strip.

AND A LEAN, SILENT FIGURE SLOWLY FADES INTO THE GATHERING DARKNESS, AWARE AT LAST THAT IN THIS WORLD, WITH GREAT POWER THERE MUST ALSO COME - - GREAT RESPONSIBILITY!

This takes the audience back to my first story. And I then follow it up with ...

Be more left and less right.

There is no mistaking that this is the end of the presentation, there is no missing the message I'm giving and there is a clear reference to the theme that I've woven throughout the talk. This ending suits my storytelling approach.

There are many other ways of ending your talk. You can end it with a call to action. You can end it with an 'answer'. You can end it with an intention or a manifesto for change. But however you do it: end positively.

HOW TO END YOUR TALK

1. A CALL TO ACTION

If you are talking about changing behaviour or campaigning in one way or another, a natural way to end is to introduce a call to action. This needs to be clear and simple. This needs to build off the tension of the story and carve a way for the audience to support you.

One of the best examples I've seen of this is Sean Carasso speaking at the Do Lectures. It is an incredibly moving talk about the Democratic Republic of the Congo and Sean uses story to great effect. He also ends with a call to action.

2. END WITH A CHOICE

If you have used oscillation as your approach then a really simple way to end is with an 'either/or' question. Do you want to live in a world like this, or like this? Do you want to live in a world of hate or love? You've already set this up in your talk and you simply end with the binary choice.

3. LESSONS LEARNED

This is probably the simplest way to end. No matter what the story is, no matter what your idea is, no matter whether it has a happy or sad ending; you can always pull out a number of lessons. The world seems to favour these things in threes, but my view is that these rules are for breaking. So, your easiest option is to pull the things out that you wished you had known before the story starts, or the condensed learning of the story. Pull them out and put them forward as lessons. Leave the most positive one until the end.

4. GIVE THE ANSWER

You plant the seeds for this one at the beginning. Start your talk with a question that you answer with your very last sentence. Your story reveals and illustrates your learning and you circle back around to answer the question right at the end.

5. SOUND BITE

Condense your talk into one simple sound bite. Perhaps the most famous of these is Steve Jobs' 'Stay hungry. Stay foolish'. It's a little like the call to action but at a philosophical rather than action level.

6. RECAP

You can recap the main points of your presentation but this can feel really clumsy, and even condescending, to me. That whole 'This is what I'm going to tell you, this is what I'm telling you, this is what I told you' approach. Consider an alternative ending.

7. A RHETORICAL QUESTION

If your talk is clear, if it builds on logic and emotion and takes the audience through to a clear point of view, then finishing with a rhetorical question can sometimes be enough. Ric Elias does just that in a haunting talk. Find it on the website.

When I plan my talks I always start with the end in mind. I ask the organisers what they want attendees and delegates to feel, think or do at the end. This is my starting point. I begin with the last box or circle on my storyboard and then go back to the first. So I begin at the end. This links back to Chapter 6, Your Audience. What do you want the audience to do afterwards? Start with this at the forefront of your mind.

You need to really hold your nerve at the end. The temptation is to fade out. Please don't. Stand centre stage, make your final point and then stay where you are. Then thank the audience and when it is time to walk off stage do it with confidence and a smile and walk slowly off. Leave with style.

Afterwards, people will want to talk to you. This is a good thing. They will want to tell you they enjoyed your talk. This is a kindness. Now, don't reject the thanks that people have queued up to give you. It's easy to get a little too modest about this stuff. To be a little British about it, apologetic almost. You know how it goes:

'You look great in that frock / top / suit / hat.'

'Oh, this old thing, I got it in the sale / found it at the back of the wardrobe / have had it for ages.'

Why? Why do we do this? Why can't we take the compliment?

Let's replay that.

> 'Thanks so much for the presentation, it really moved / changed / inspired me.'

> *'Oh, that old thing, I found it at the back of my laptop / bought it cheap from someone else / wrote it ages ago.'*

If people have waited in line, have found the courage to talk to you, have made the effort to see you, then at least acknowledge what they have said. The other half of the giving equation is receiving.

But don't punch the air and shout, 'Yes, I'm the boss!' A little modesty goes a long way.

10
MOVING OFF THE STAGE AND INTO LIFE

It won't have escaped your attention that much of this book's content can be applied to other parts of life. The tips and techniques, the approaches and practices, are as much about finding calm, finding your strength, finding your story, quieting your mind, and reclaiming your voice.

In this book we've looked at presenting in front of an audience, but what about when we're not on stage? The way we portray ourselves to others has changed significantly over the last ten years. Sure, social media has been a big part of this shift. We see further into people's lives now than we have ever done. Or we think we do. The problem is that, for many, this is acting not being.

We compare our 'being' with their acting and that's a comparison that's a little unbalanced.

My hope is that this book has shown you how to present authentically in a world that is often inauthentic, a world where businesses curate what we see about them, and where individuals are now doing the same. This curation is not always authentic. It is often acting. Some of my best friends act all the time. They portray an image of themselves that is a fabrication; if you talk to the people that work for them you'll find it is nothing other than a projection; if you sit down with them for a cup of tea it melts away and the real them is struggling like everyone else is struggling. We often want to pretend to be something that we aren't because we don't like what we are, what we have become. This is common, so please don't worry if this hits home. The problem with a world that is becoming so inauthentic is that it's hard to recognise real authenticity sometimes. The opportunity here is that real authenticity is so rare, if you can communicate it you will *soar*.

There are many lessons from this book that you can take with you into the rest of your life. These are summarised below:

1. UNDERSTAND YOUR WHY

What are you for? Why do you get out of bed in the morning and why should anyone care? This is a tricky and philosophical point that will hit you sometime in your life. My advice is to think this one through earlier rather than later. What do you care about, I mean *really* care about? Not money. We all need enough money. We all need enough to survive, even thrive. But what pursuit will result in this bounty? My advice is not to chase money but to chase good work. You will find that money chases you this way. What is it that fills your soul with fire and your heart with joy? What is it that you'd really like to do 'if you had your time again'? What do you believe in? This is the place to start. This is the thing to focus upon first, and although it's an old idea there is no sell-by date on great ideas. What would you do with your life if you knew how long you had left? What do you want to tell your kids / grandkids / nephews and nieces that you did? Go and do that.

2. LEARN TO LIKE YOURSELF

No, fuck it. Learn to *love* yourself. Nothing good comes from self-loathing, nothing good comes from serious self-deprecation. The benefits of the freedom of actually liking, loving and being proud of yourself are massive and will stay with you for life. Spend more time with yourself and avoid activities that stop you doing this. It is really easy to keep running. To keep moving. To not sit. But what are you running from? There is a great song by Gil Scott Heron called 'Running' and my favourite line is:

"*I ALWAYS FEEL LIKE RUNNING, NOT AWAY BECAUSE THERE'S NO SUCH PLACE*"

And that's the truth. Away has gone away. Sometimes you just need to stop and look in the mirror. Do you like what you see? If not, change who you are. This starts with understanding who you are and that starts with gentle introspection, but it doesn't need to be meditation. It could be any solo activity (running, swimming, etc.) Anything that leaves you with yourself. Of course, meditation and yoga are both great here, but you do what you like.

3. LEARN TO LOOK AFTER YOURSELF

You all know the advice you get in the safety briefing on a plane:

'If we experience a drop in pressure, oxygen masks will fall from the ceiling. Please fit your own before helping others to fit theirs.'

This is true. If you aren't well, how are you going to care for those you are looking out for? So learn to look after yourself. There are a few simple things that can help here:

Sleep

Sleep is so very important and we have (until relatively recently) taken a very dismissive approach to it. You know the sort of thing: 'sleep is for wimps', 'I only need about four hours', 'sleep is a waste of time'. But sleep science has accelerated massively in the last year or so. We now understand more about sleep cycles and this has revealed the myth of eight hours' sleep a night. In his book *Sleep*, Nick Littlehales explains about 90-minute cycles of sleep. Getting five of these cycles in each night is the key. They don't all need to be together. For me this has taken the panic of insomnia away. If I wake at 3 am, it's fine. I've had three 90-minute cycles by then, I only need two more (and I know I can perform on four cycles as long as this only occurs twice a week).

It sounds crazy that I'm running the calculations during the night, but one of the biggest problems I have with sleep is the fear that I'm not getting enough, that I'll wake up and not get back off to sleep. This knowledge has removed that fear.

Sleep is your friend. The science is really clear now. Good sleep practice can reduce stress, enhance cognition, strengthens the immune system, aids mood, improves concentration, enhances memory, reduces the risk of high blood pressure and coronary heart disease, reduces the risk of diabetes, and can help improve your relationships.

Sleep well. You'll do a better presentation the next day. Sleep is a key element of brain health, of mental clarity, and therefore of your performance.

Exercise

All through this book I have extolled the virtues of exercise in terms of better and sharper thinking. Clearly there are significant physical benefits too. I'm not going to list them here but if you want a healthy heart, body and brain then you need to move more.

Food

Just eat less harm. Harm to you, to the planet and to animals. I'm not preaching veganism here, or telling you to stop having treats, or avoiding food that has a massive environmental impact; I'm preaching moderation. You are what you eat, so eat better things.

Mental health

We all suffer at times. We all get a bit glum. We all get a bit stressed. Some more than others. The key thing here is to talk about it. Have enough people around you that care about you and talk to them. But remember to be there when they want to talk to you. It's a two-way street.

4. KNOW YOUR LIMITING BELIEFS

My guess is that this bit in the book poked some of you quite hard. My guess is that the bit about limiting beliefs made some of you see yours for the first time. Look, don't worry. We all have them. I mean all of us. I hear things like 'I'm just not that kind of person' (yeah, but you could be); 'I can't present like you' (no, but you can present like *you*); 'I'm just not that creative' (yes, you are); I hear it all the time. Every session I run. And as Henry Ford said, the truth is:

"WHETHER YOU THINK YOU CAN OR YOU THINK YOU CAN'T, YOU ARE RIGHT."

Just think about it: Why would you set your own barriers? The world is queueing up to erect barriers for you, to put you in a box. Why make it easier? Understanding the framework of thinking that sits behind your limiting beliefs is important. Your limiting beliefs are essentially there to protect you, to keep you safe. But at some point they outstay their welcome and they only serve to keep you small. It is tempting to delve into who gave you them (it could be yourself, of course). Don't spend too long there. Work it out, thank them, wish them well, move on.

5. SAY YES MORE

To presentations, of course, but to many things in life. Put yourself out there. The only way you will get better at presenting is to present more. The only way you will get used to standing in front of people is to do it more. The only way your voice will be heard is if you use it more.

6. ENJOY THINGS

Happiness is a choice. I once had a business partner who was unhappy. Always seeing the negative, always glum. I tried to make him happier. But then I realised that he was happy being the unhappy one. That was his role and he loved it. That's just fine. Well, it was for him, not so much for me. It's really hard to be around someone who revels in that role, who likes that role so much that they become that role.

Every morning you get up and have a choice: how will you greet the day today? Will you greet it with a smile or a scowl? Sure, things will happen that will make you scowl or smile, but if your default position is a smile my guess is that you'll have a better day. I have a mantra that I stole off my friend Anna in California. It is:

GRUMPY TO GRATITUDE

If something makes me grumpy, doesn't go my way, I try and find the good in the situation. I try and move from grumpy to gratitude. If I can't find anything positive in the situation then I think more generally about my life and the things I'm grateful for.

Not everything in the garden is rosy but starting out trying to see the good in things takes you further than starting with the bad.

7. YOU ARE BEAUTIFUL

You are. You truly are. You got born against the odds. You survived school. You survived the teenage years. You wake up every morning and you take a breath. You hopefully are able to feel the electricity when you hold the hands of the people you love. I sit writing this at the age of 51. I've spent too long worrying about stuff that never happened, people that didn't like me but didn't matter. You are beautiful.

8. THIS IS NOT AN ACT

But it is a performance. Not just your talk, but your life. Dance like you did at eighteen. Sing like you did at eight. Love like it is your last days. Run like the wind.

And finally, I was lucky enough to deliver a talk at the brilliant The Good Life Experience a week after my 50th birthday. The talk was called 'Kindness is a Competitive Advantage'. It was really moving. I'd found out the night before that I was going to be a grandfather; the talk was emotionally charged; and more people squeezed in to hear my talk than they had at any talk before. I was fighting back the emotions that came in waves. I delivered a great talk (that's not ego, that's knowing when you're on fire). For the talk, I pulled together 25 things that I've learned in my 50 years. I repeat them here as some of them are nice.

1. **Be kind. There are enough arses in the world already. Team Arse do not need another member.**

2. **You are good enough. You are not: too fat, too old, too busy, too tired, too late. Only the last one matters. Don't be too late.**

3. **When you change, some people won't like it. Some will undermine you, some will criticise, some will disappear. This isn't about you. This is about them and their fears.**

4. **You look amazing when you feel confident.**

5. **Being still is as important as moving.**

6. **Listening is as important as talking.**

7. **Don't just talk about it, do it.**

8. **Don't believe your own press; stay humble.**

9. **Jump in cold water often.**

10. **Get sweaty often.**

11. **Everyone has imposter syndrome.**

12. **Love with all your heart.**

13. **Money matters: having too little gets in the way, but having too much gets in the way too.**

14. **If you make a deal with someone stick to it, or they won't make a deal with you again.**

15. **Sleep well.**

16. **Eat less harm.**

17. **Yoga is magic.**

18. **Love is your friend but if you chase it then it will become as elusive as the rainbow's end.**

19. **If you think it then it is more likely to happen.**

20. **Everyone is creative.**

21. **Success is as scary as failure.**

22. **You are the average of the people you hang around with.**

23. **Health and opportunity can't be recycled, don't fritter them away.**

24. **Being scared is the worst reason for not doing something.**

25. **Believe in something bigger than you.**

26. **With power comes responsibility.**

27. **Smile, it's free.**

28. **Dance more.**

Okay, I lied. There are 28.

WE ALL HAVE A VOICE.
WE ALL HAVE
A STORY TO TELL.
GO AND TELL YOURS,
AS NO ONE ELSE
WILL TELL IT FOR YOU.

POSTSCRIPT

This book came out in the spring of 2020, when a global pandemic hit and every event around the world was cancelled. As someone who earned most of their income from presenting to lots of people in the same room or running workshops, this was a scary time. It was also not the best time to launch a book on public speaking. Despite that, the book held its own and gradually things started to move online.

The most popular platform was Zoom, as well as Microsoft Teams, Webex and GoTo. They all present the same challenges, most notably how to appear human via a technology that removes personality, flattens tone of voice, and makes smiles and facial gesticulation harder to read. These platforms were not meant for full presentations and conferences, but they were designed for group events and have been used really well by some. One great example is fellow Do Book author James Sills and his Sofa Singers initiative.

There are a number of challenges that arise from the technology but on the whole, it makes our lives better and these tools and platforms are now an essential part of most businesses. This postscript looks at a few simple tips that you can apply when presenting online.

ZOOM IS YOUR ROOM

People will see you and they will see your environment. No matter how you live, what your home office is like, make sure they see the bit you want them to see. For example, my studio is in the garden. They don't need to know that I use the space as a cycle studio too. I set the laptop or camera up to accordingly. It may be a bit of a pain but five minutes setting-up your space is time well spent.

It is important to think about the device that you will be using. A laptop rarely gives the most flattering angle. It tends to be too low and makes your chin look like, well, chins. Very simply, perch your laptop on some books or use a laptop stand. If you use a tablet or phone with a stand ensure that this is tightened-up. I once started a live qi gong session and my iPad slowly tipped forward until all you could see were my feet. Now, I think I've got okay feet, but they're not for broadcast.

STANDING OR SITTING?

How do you want to present? How do you feel more comfortable? I much prefer standing to sitting so I will always stand when possible. I move around and I use that movement to convey energy, enthusiasm and passion. It's important to see my head, feet and about a metre each side of me. So, spend time creating your frame.

QUESTIONS

Questions can be asked on all the online platforms. Seeing them arrive can be a distraction and interrupt your flow. Where possible, have someone else review the questions, maybe one of the organisers or someone that works with you. Get them to pull out the best ones.

Alternatively, drag the questions and comments box into a separate screen. This keeps them out of the way until you need them, you can also enlarge them or shrink them.

ENGAGEMENT

Engagement is one of the hardest things to do virtually. In-person you can feel someone's charisma, their magnetism, their confidence. Over a screen these things can be misunderstood as arrogance. Remember that you need to be yourself, not anyone else. But more than ever you need to be a bigger version of yourself. This doesn't mean being brash or overconfident, just slightly more animated than normal. But don't overdo it. We are looking for 10 per cent more you, not 100 per cent. Rapport is so much harder when presenting this way, so remember to smile, listen and stay engaged. If you normally ask questions during your presentations, you can still do this but if there is a decent-sized audience, think carefully about the phrasing. You really need yes/no or thumbs-up/thumbs-down responses.

SOUND

A presentation without a picture is better than one without sound. Help your audience out. Either get close to the microphone, connect an external one, or use headphones to improve sound quality. Turn on the 'natural sound' options and turn off modulated sound. Sound modulation distorts the voice like early autotune on pop songs. You don't need it.

Remember to mute everyone's microphone apart from the person managing the chat box and yours. Turn your email notification off. No one wants to hear your pings. In fact, be on the safe side and shut down every programme other than the one you are using.

BREATHING

It's as important to think about your breathing here, as when you are on stage. Sit up straight or stand up. When you sit there is a tendency to curve a little and this restricts your lung capacity and the amount you breathe in. When speaking there is a greater tendency to mouth-breathe, which can often result in taking in too much oxygen. I have had to work really hard to slow my breathing, to breathe through my nose. Not only does this sound less 'panty', it also has the effect of reducing our heart rate and in turn, panic and anxiety.

FINAL CHECKS

Okay, your room looks great, you take your position and turn on your camera only to realise ... you have spinach in your teeth ... you forgot to do your hair ... You are about to be screen-size. This is much bigger than you ever are on stage. Spend a couple of minutes making sure that you look presentable — however that is. Then it may sound obvious but make sure you have entered the correct platform/room/code. The last thing you want is to be sat in the wrong waiting room on Teams when everyone else is on Zoom.

Lastly, how will people remember you? What can you leave them with that will help them understand your ideas more clearly? You have an opportunity to share something tangible with them via a link in the chat to everyone watching.

While nothing beats face-to-face experiences, sometimes travel, time or cost get in the way. Events will continue to be livestreamed and presentations made online. Digital conferences will continue to grow and, while the core lessons of this book still apply, it is worth considering the additional elements in this chapter to help you fly.

APPENDIX

LIST OF VALUES

It's hard to work out what you stand for, but if you stand for nothing you'll fall for anything. These values, traits and themes are a starter for ten. Pick eight that you align with. Then whittle them down to three. That's the start of working out what you stand for.

Trust	Rewarding	Support
Innovation	Completion	Love
Exciting	Success	Tireless
Adding value	Attention	Contribution
Money	Appreciation	Doing good
Freedom	Fighting spirt	Out of comfort zone
Help people	Fulfilment	Freedom
Empathy	Sharing	Democracy
Move people	Wellbeing	Morals
Learning	Health	Control
Innovative	Passion	Trust
Giving	Fun	Security
Happy	Cerebral	Making a difference
Change seeking	Challenge	Energising
Open	Stretches	Nourishing
Problem solving	New directions	Sharing
Creativity	Pushing	Hunger
Family	Energised	Trust
Communication	Respect	Curiosity
Engaging	Excited by others	

STORYBOARD TEMPLATES

Plan your presentation using these templates. In each box pop a word or a picture that sums up a segment of the talk. These are your stories. You know them.

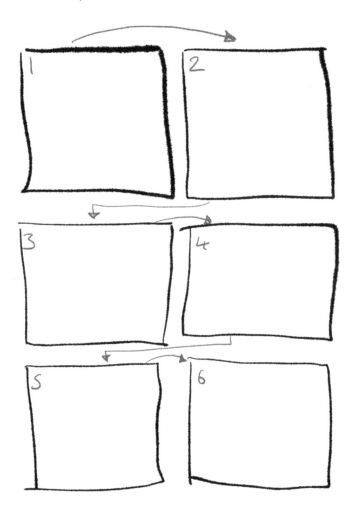

This way you only need to remember six things, not everything.
If you prefer a more organic approach use this circles template.

Any order, any direction.

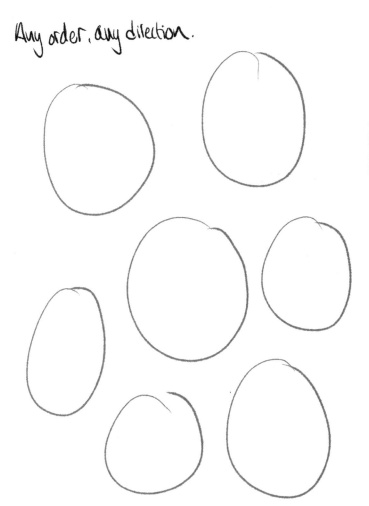

ABOUT THE AUTHOR

Mark Shayler is one of Britain's most charismatic keynote speakers. He has made a reputation by thinking on his feet and engaging audiences all over the globe. He has spoken to some of the world's biggest organisations. When he isn't on stage, he is a leading change consultant for companies including Amazon, Samsung, Coca-Cola, Unilever and John Lewis. He is a founding partner of the Do Lectures, and the author of *Do Disrupt: Change the status quo. Or become it.* (Do Books, 2013).

THANKS

A massive thanks to David and Clare Hieatt for starting the Do Lectures and inviting me to come up with a workshop that become the Do Present workshop — and is now a book. Thanks for helping me help others find a voice. Thanks also go to Miranda West for having the foresight to start the Do Book Company and for trusting me with one of the very first books back in 2013 (*Do Disrupt*) and now this one. Indeed, thanks to the entire team at Do Books.

As you wander through life you encounter incredible teachers. I have been lucky in attracting great talent to teach me. In no particular order thanks go to: Mr Spencer, Doug Jeffries, Nigel Copperthwaite, Dai Larner, The Stone Roses, Tom Dolman, Public Enemy, Keith Warren, Steve Manifold, Guy Shayler, Andy Middleton, Charlie Gladstone, James Victore, Nicola Shayler, Nick Drake, Gil Scott Heron, Mr Ralf, the late John Roberts.

I'm really lucky to still see my school mates regularly. I've known some of these since I was six years old. So, thanks to the Purple Y-Fronts (Keith, Allan, Marc, Bert, Pete, Jon and Neil), Stuart Jordan and Gary Teb.

When I was about 43, I decided to do something pretty scary. It is a weekend run by the Mankind Project in the UK. I think it was called New Warrior Training. It was hard.

I was shitting myself. I was worried I would make an excuse
not to go, so I arranged to pick up several other men at
designated train stations en route to the venue. It was a
smart move. The first man I met at the train station was
Waqar Siraj. A beautiful soul and one of my best friends
to this day. Aho, brother.

Then there is my family. My grandparents were all
amazing and are all dead, but I thank them for my genes,
particularly the ones that allow me to still kick a drop-goal
from 40 metres out. My parents were, and still are, great
parents. Kind, giving, firm, supportive, proud, loving.
The skill of parenting is making it up as you go along but
looking like there is a plan there. My brother Guy means
more to me than he knows. Thanks, bro.

Then there's Team Shayler. I properly met my wife,
Nic, in the back of a rough nightclub behind a pub in a
town called Hinckley. I'd seen her once or twice before
and was already utterly in love but we'd never spoken.
I thought she was out of my league. But through the dry
ice, through the clouds of cheap perfume mixed with the
smell of hair gel, testosterone and spot cream, I knew she
was the one. That night we got talking after she 'nudged'
the girl I was chatting up off a stool to take her place. It was
all romance and letters. Snogging and urgency. Love and
sex. Marriage and university. Friends and wine. Babies
and bliss. Babies and babies. And then the fourth baby.
My four kids are simply astonishing and teach me more
than I could ever teach them.

You are all remarkable people. Thank you.

Books in the series

Also available

Available in print, digital and audio formats from booksellers or via our website: **thedobook.co**

To hear about events and forthcoming titles, you can find us on social media @dobookco, or subscribe to our newsletter